EASTERN CHEROKEE CENSUS
CHEROKEE, NORTH CAROLINA
1915 - 1922
TAKEN BY AGENT JAMES E. HENDERSON

VOLUME I
1915-1916

TRANSCRIBED BY
JEFF BOWEN

NATIVE STUDY
Gallipolis, Ohio
USA

Other Books and Series by Jeff Bowen

1901-1907 Native American Census Seneca, Eastern Shawnee, Miami, Modoc, Ottawa, Peoria, Quapaw, and Wyandotte Indians (Under Seneca School, Indian Territory)

1932 Census of The Standing Rock Sioux Reservation with Births And Deaths 1924-1932

Census of The Blackfeet, Montana, 1897- 1901 Expanded Edition

Eastern Cherokee by Blood, 1906-1910, Volumes I thru XIII

Choctaw of Mississippi Indian Census 1929-1932 with Births and Deaths 1924-1931 Volume I

Choctaw of Mississippi Indian Census 1933, 1934 & 1937, Supplemental Rolls to 1934 & 1935 with Births and Deaths 1932-1938, and Marriages 1936-1938 Volume II

Eastern Cherokee Census Cherokee, North Carolina 1930-1939 Census 1930-1931 with Births And Deaths 1924-1931 Taken By Agent L. W. Page Volume I

Eastern Cherokee Census Cherokee, North Carolina 1930-1939 Census 1932-1933 with Births And Deaths 1930-1932 Taken By Agent R. L. Spalsbury Volume II

Eastern Cherokee Census Cherokee, North Carolina 1930-1939 Census 1934-1937 with Births and Deaths 1925-1938 and Marriages 1936 & 1938 Taken by Agents R. L. Spalsbury And Harold W. Foght Volume III

Seminole of Florida Indian Census, 1930-1940 with Birth and Death Records, 1930-1938

Texas Cherokees 1820-1839 A Document For Litigation 1921

Choctaw By Blood Enrollment Cards 1898-1914 Volumes I thru XVII

Starr Roll 1894 (Cherokee Payment Rolls) Districts: Canadian, Cooweescoowee, and Delaware Volume One

Starr Roll 1894 (Cherokee Payment Rolls) Districts: Flint, Going Snake, and Illinois Volume Two

Starr Roll 1894 (Cherokee Payment Rolls) Districts: Saline, Sequoyah, and Tahlequah; Including Orphan Roll Volume Three

Other Books and Series by Jeff Bowen

Cherokee Intruder Cases Dockets of Hearings 1901-1909 Volumes I & II

Indian Wills, 1911-1921 Records of the Bureau of Indian Affairs
Books One thru Seven;

Native American Wills & Probate Records 1911-1921

Turtle Mountain Reservation Chippewa Indians 1932 Census with Births & Deaths, 1924-1932

Chickasaw By Blood Enrollment Cards 1898-1914 Volume I thru V

Cherokee Descendants East An Index to the Guion Miller Applications Volume I
Cherokee Descendants West An Index to the Guion Miller Applications Volume II (A-M)
Cherokee Descendants West An Index to the Guion Miller Applications Volume III (N-Z)

Applications for Enrollment of Seminole Newborn Freedmen, Act of 1905

Visit our website at **www.nativestudy.com** to learn more about these and other books and series by Jeff Bowen

Originally published:
Baltimore, Maryland
2004

Reprinted by:

Native Study LLC
Gallipolis, OH
www.nativestudy.com
2020

Library of Congress Control Number: 2020916205

ISBN: 978-1-64968-044-0

Made in the United States of America.

This series is dedicated to
David West
a friend for whom I will always be thankful.

INTRODUCTION

This is a transcription of the census of the Eastern Band of Cherokee Indians taken by James E. Henderson, Indian Agent representing the United States for the Bureau of Indian Affairs. The transcription covers the eight years between 1915 and 1922 and is based on a microfilm copy of a typescript originally on file at the National Archives in Washington, D.C.* The census taker probably went to the reservation, took the census in his own hand, then delivered it to Washington, where it was alphabetized, typed up, and subsequently microfilmed. This present transcription, published in four volumes (two census years per volume) marks the first time this material has been made available as a publication.

The format employed by the census taker changed from year to year, first in small matters, then in more important details. For instance, at the conclusion of the 1915 census there is a summary statement of the total number of individuals in various age and sex groups, but in 1916 and later censuses there is no such summary statement. The "RECEIVED" stamp appeared on the census for a few years, but it too was eventually dropped. Towards the last few years of the census there were more significant changes--sometimes the information included birth and death dates or the names of children living apart from their parents or references to an individual's marital status.

In most cases the information provided in this census is self-explanatory, although family relationships are not always easy to figure out, despite the fact that every individual enumerated is identified by a qualifier such as "husb" or "wife" or "dau" or "son." Where there are discrepancies and anomalies, I can only say that I have transcribed the data exactly as it appears in the microfilm and idiosyncracies in my text are characteristic of the microfilmed typescript, which in turn reflects the methodology of the census taker. In my judgment it is better to have a verbatim transcript of the census than a version that is based on interpretation and flawed conclusions.

The census itself concerns the Eastern Band of Cherokee Indians from Cherokee, North Carolina, living on the reservation known as the Qualla Boundary. Individuals enumerated in the census are descendants of the Cherokees who were *not* removed to Indian Territory during the period 1838-39 in the migration known as the Trail of Tears. While there is sometimes additional data, information provided in the census almost invariably gives the individual's name, family relationship, date of birth, and sex--information that is critical in any genealogical research.

Jeff Bowen
Gallipolis, Ohio
NativeStudy.com

*Microfilm Roll M595-23, Native American Census Rolls 1885-1940.

ADDENDUM

Addendum to the previous printing of this volume it was decided that it was better for this series to have a limited index rather than a full index because most of the work is already in alphabetical order.

CENSUS ROLL

of

EASTERN BAND
OF
CHEROKEE INDIANS

1915

North Carolina Eastern Cherokee Census 1915-1922
June 30,1915   Taken by: James E. Henderson
1915-1916   Volume I

Roll Number	English Name	Relationship	Date of Birth	Sex
1	Ahnetonah, Nancy	Widow	1837	F
2	Allen, Will	Husb	1845	M
3	" Sallie	Wife	1851	F
4	" John	Husb	1871	M
5	" Eve	Wife	1884	F
6	Welch, Emeline	Stp Dau	1901	F
7	Allison, Nannie I	Wife	1883	F
8	" Roy Robert	Son	1904	M
9	" Albert Monroe	Son	1907	M
10	" Ida May	Dau	1909	F
11	" Felix Wilbur	Son	1912	M
12	" Boyce Jackson	Son	1914	M
13	Anderson, Addie LG	Wife	1889	F
14	" Girtie	Dau	1910	F
15	" Louisa Jane	Wife	1879	F
16	" Bessie	Dau	1902	F
17	" Cora	Dau	1904	F
18	" Ella	Dau	1910	F
19	" William Burl	Son	1912	M
20	Arch, David	Husb	1859	M
21	" Martha	Wife	1884	F
22	" Ross	Son	1896	M
23	" Jess	Son	1908	M
24	" Jimmie	Son	1910	M
25	" Eva Stella	Dau	1911	F
26	Arch, Olivan	Dau	1894	F
27	" Saunooke Steve	Ward	1897	M
28	" Arch, Johnson	Husb	1884	M
29	" Ella	Wife	1890	F
30	" Cora	Dau	1908	F
31	" Harach	Son	1909	M
32	" Elma	Dau	1911	F
33	" ? Baby	Dau	1915	F
34	Armachain, Amy	Seprt Wife	1849	F
35	" Lacy	Husb	1876	M
36	" Anna	Wife	1875	F
37	" James	Son	1909	M
38	" Davis	Husb	1855	M
39	" Annie	Wife	1871	F
40	" Jess	Son	1896	M
41	" Louis	Son	1898	M
42	" Rachel	Dau	1901	F
43	" Sevier	Son	1904	M
44	" Chewonih	Seprt Husb	1844	M
45	Arneach, Will West	Widr	1849	M

Roll Number	English Name	Relationship	Date of Birth	Sex
46	" Nellie West	Dau	1896	F
47	" Buck West	Son	1894	M
48	" Jefferson	Husb	1874	M
49	" Sarah	Wife	1875	F
50	" Margaret	Dau	1906	F
51	Arneach, Samuel	Son	1909	M
52	" John EH	Son	1911	M
53	" Sylvester Stilwel	Son	1914	M
54	" Stella Pocahontas	Dau	1913	F
55	Bird, Lizzie	St-Dau	1899	F
56	" Bessie	St-Dau	1901	F
57	" David	St-Son	1894	M
58	Axe, Willie	Wid	1871	M
59	" Maggie	Dau	1895	F
60	" Sarah	Dau	1896	F
61	" John D	Husb	1854	M
62	" Eve	Wife	1864	F
63	" Josiah	Husb	1864	M
64	" Sarah	Wife	1881	F
65	" Nancy	Dau	1903	F
66	" Ella	Dau	1905	F
67	" Corinthia	Dau	1907	F
68	" Lazrus	Son	1909	M
69	" Lula	Dau	1910	F
70	" Dora	Dau	1913	F
71	" Cindy	Dau	1890	F
72	Baker, Elmira	Wife	1872	F
73	" Dona	Dau	1895	F
74	" Crickett	Son	1904	M
75	" Ben	Son	1905	M
76	Baker, Ada	Dau	1909	F
77	" Homer	Son	1912	M
78	" Luther	Son	1893	M
79	" Ella C Bruce	Wife	1862	F
80	" Ella McCoy	Wife	1878	F
81	" Stella	Dau	1898	F
82	" Charley W	Son	1902	M
83	" Mary R	Dau	1905	F
84	" Cora	Dau	1910	F
85	" Alice	Dau	1913	F
86	Bates, Deliah W Smith	Wife	1870	F
87	" Marshall Smith	Son	1897	M
88	" Lizzie	Dau	1902	F
89	Winkler, Selina S	Wife	1894	F
90	Batson, Henrietta Crow	Wife	1887	F

Roll Number	English Name	Relationship	Date of Birth	Sex
91	" Alfred G	Son	1911	M
92	" Olivan Jane	Dau	1914	F
93	Bearmeat, Mary	Wid	1845	F
94	Ben, Cheick	Husb	1865	M
95	" Ollie	Wife	1884	F
96	" James	Son	1904	M
97	" Olivan	Dau	1906	F
98	" Candy	Son	1911	M
99	" Callie	Dau	1913	F
100	Bigmeat, Robert	Son	1894	M
101	Bigmeat, Charlotte L Crow	Wife	------	F
102	" Minnie Crow	Dau	1913	F
103	" Nicodemus	Husb	1875	M
104	" Nannie	Wife	1865	F
105	" Yona	Son	1877	M
106	" Ainihkih	Wid	1848	M
107	" Adam	Son	1891	M
108	" Isiah	Husb	1878	M
109	" Sarah	Wife	1882	F
110	" John	Son	1912	M
111	Bird, Timpson	Son	1885	M
112	" Squainchi	Husb	1845	M
113	" Ollie	Seprt Wife	1882	F
114	" Annie	Dau	1906	F
115	" Lucy	Dau	1909	F
116	" Minnie Peckerwood	Dau	1911	F
117	" Joe	Son	1913	M
118	" Lloyd	Seprt Husb	1883	M
119	" Stephen	Husb	1853	M
120	" Annie	Wife	1856	F
121	" Teheskie	Husb	1840	M
122	" Celia	Wife	1853	M
123	" Going	Husb	1869	M
124	" Annie	Wife	1864	F
125	Tooni, Garfield	Ward	1906	M
126	Bird, Eli	Son	1893	M
127	Blackfox, Cindy	Wid	1842	F
128	" Charley	Husb	1879	M
129	" Nancy	Wife	1883	F
130	" Lloyd	Son	1903	M
131	" Nancy	Dau	1912	F
132	" Josiah	Husb	1851	M
133	" Dinah G	Wife	1857	F
134	" Keziah	Step Son	1895	M
135	Blankenship, Arizona	Wife	1875	F

Roll Number		English Name	Relationship	Date of Birth	Sex
136	"	Lillie J	Dau	1909	F
137	"	Fred	Son	1911	M
138	"	LeRoy Edwin	Son	1915	M
139	"	Helen Kathalene	Dau	1913	F
140	Blue Owl		Wid	1858	M
141	Blythe, Arch		Husb	1877	M
142	Blythe, Ida		Wife	1881	F
143	"	Sampson	Son	1904	M
144	"	Birdie Bell	Dau	1910	F
145	"	Francis Marion	Son	1913	M
146	"	William Henry	Bach	1876	M
147	"	James	Wid	1861	M
148	Bauer, Fred		Ward	1897	M
149	"	Owena	Ward	1895	F
150	Blythe, Jarrett		Husb	1886	M
151	Blythe, Mary B		Wife	1893	F
152	"	David	Husb	1862	M
153	"	Nancy	Wife	1874	F
154	"	William Johnson	Husb	1872	M
155	"	Lloyd	Son	1909	M
156	Crow, Louisa		St-Dau	1904	F
157	Blythe, Allen		Son	1912	M
158	Bradley, Henry		Husb	1884	M
159	"	Nancy	Wife	1881	F
160	"	James	Son	1906	M
161	"	Nancy	Dau	1908	F
162	"	Dewesee	Son	1909	M
163	"	Shon	Son	1911	M
164	George, Goliath		St-Son	1902	M
165	Bradley, Eliza Jane		Wife	1872	F
166	"	Amos	Son	1896	M
167	"	Henry	Son	1900	M
168	"	Judson	Son	1902	M
169	"	Lydia	Dau	1905	F
170	"	Seaborn	Son	1907	M
171	"	Bertha Ann	Dau	1910	F
172	"	Wallace Russell	Son	1912	M
173	"	Nancy	Dau	1876	F
174	"	Margaret	Dau	1899	F
175	"	Roy	Son	1905	M
176	Bradley, Minda		Dau	1905	F
177	"	Verdie Winterfr'd	Dau	1909	F
178	"	Annie	Dau	1902	F
179	"	Dinah	Dau	1903	F
180	"	Rachel	Dau	1906	F

North Carolina Eastern Cherokee Census 1915-1922
June 30,1915   Taken by: James E. Henderson
1915-1916   Volume I

Roll Number		English Name	Relationship	Date of Birth	Sex
181	"	Thomas	Son	1908	M
182	"	Martha I	Dau	1914	F
183	"	Bradley, Joseph	Husb	1881	M
184	"	Bettie	Dau	1915	F
185	"	Johnson	Son	1909	M
186	"	Lucinda	Dau	1912	F
187	"	Lewis	Son	1913	M
188	"	Walter	Son	1902	M
189	"	Nick	Son	1895	M
190	"	Morgan	Son	1892	M
191	"	Sarah	Husb	1879	M
192	"	Johnson	Husb	1879	M
193	"	Ethel	Dau	1910	F
194	"	Antoin Russel	Son	1912	M
195		Brady, Susie Smith	Wife	1886	F
196	"	James Lowen	Son	1910	M
197	"	Samuel	Son	1912	M
198	"	William	Son	1915	M
199	"	Robert A	Husb	1868	M
200	"	Eliza	Dau	1895	F
201		Brady, Sarah	Dau	1897	F
202	"	Arthur	Son	1899	M
203	"	McKinley	Son	1902	M
204	"	Luther	Son	1904	M
205	"	Elizabeth	Dau	1907	F
206	"	Clyde	Son	1908	M
207	"	Callie	Dau	1911	F
208		Brewster, Linnie L Jordan	Wife	1892	F
209	"	Elly	Dau	1910	F
210		Brown, Lydia	Wid	1847	F
211	"	Peter	Div-Husb	1883	M
212	"	Nancy	Div-Wife	1883	F
213	"	Jonah	Husb	1881	M
214	"	Agnes	Wife	1881	F
215	"	Mark	Son	1910	M
216	"	Lizzie	Dau	1912	F
217		Bruce, Arthur	Husb	1890	M
218	"	Thomas	Husb	1886	M
219		Bryant, Elizabeth HG	Wife	1861	F
220		Burgess, Georgia Ann	Wife	1869	F
221	"	Bessie L	Dau	1896	F
222	"	R Floy	Dau	1899	F
223	"	Willie R	Son	1902	M
224	"	George Alger	Son	1906	M
225	"	Nellie Luella	Dau	1909	F

Roll Number	English Name	Relationship	Date of Birth	Sex
226	Burgess, Homer Frederick	Son	1911	M
227	Bushyhead, Ben	Husb	1886	M
228	" Nancy	Wife	1887	F
229	" Joel	Son	1911	M
230	" Robert	Son	1914	M
231	Callaway, Bessie M Nick	Wife	1887	F
232	Calhoun, Morgan	Husb	1864	M
233	" Sallie Ann	Wife	1877	F
234	" Eve	Dau	1898	F
235	" Yihginneh	Dau	1900	F
236	" Lawson	Son	1902	M
237	" Holly	Son	1904	M
238	" Sunday	Son	1906	M
239	" Diana	Dau	1910	F
240	" Smathers	Son	1912	M
241	" Polly	Dau	1894	F
242	" Lawyer	Husb	1859	M
243	" Ollie	Wife	1871	F
244	Cannaut, Abel	Husb	1880	M
245	" Susie	Wife	1888	F
246	" Columbus	Husb	1884	M
247	" Maggie	Div-Wife	1890	F
248	" Minnie Goforth	Wife	1887	F
249	Goforth, Louisa	St-Dau	1909	F
250	" Arthur	St-Son	1911	M
251	Cannaut, Addison	Son	1909	M
252	Cat, Ben	Husb	1867	M
253	" Oney	Wife	1860	F
254	" Johnson	Husb	1859	M
255	" Sally	Wife	1861	F
256	" Jesse	Son	1895	M
257	" Amanda	Dau	1900	F
258	Hornbuckle, Andy	Ward	1904	M
259	" Johnson	Ward	1900	M
260	Cat, Willie	Husb	1887	M
261	" Corinthia	Wife	1890	F
262	" David	Son	1909	M
263	" Robert	Son	1911	M
264	" Margaret	Dau	1891	F
265	Catolster, Eve	Wid	1842	F
266	" Wallace	Husb	1875	M
267	" Elsie Feather	Wife	1878	F
268	" Eliza	Dau	1913	F
269	" William	Son	1879	M
270	" Carson	Husb	1881	M

North Carolina Eastern Cherokee Census 1915-1922
June 30,1915   Taken by: James E. Henderson
1915-1916   Volume I

Roll Number	English Name	Relationship	Date of Birth	Sex
271	" Josie	Wife	1891	F
272	" Johnson	Son	1901	M
273	" David	Son	1910	M
274	" Margaret	Dau	1914	F
275	" Sally	Wife	1886	F
276	Catolster, Eliza Jane	Dau	1904	F
277	" Alexander	Son	1906	M
278	" Nannie	Dau	1909	F
279	" Guion M	Son	1910	M
280	" Lucy	Dau	1913	F
281	Clearly, Lucy Emeline	Wife	1879	F
282	" William Luther	Son	1900	M
283	" Emery Lorenzo	Son	1903	M
284	" Robert Astor	Son	1905	M
285	" John Patrick	Son	1911	M
286	Chekelelee, Stone	Husb	1872	M
287	" Mary	Wife	1863	F
288	" Simon	Son	1899	M
289	" Rosa	Dau	1904	F
290	" Andy	Husb	1884	M
291	" Bettie	Wife	1889	F
292	" Bessie	Dau	1910	F
293	" Martin	Son	1912	M
294	" Tom	Husb	1866	M
295	" Luella	Dau	1905	F
296	" Wilson	Son	1909	M
297	Childers, Lula Frances	Wife	1882	F
298	" Robert	Son	1905	M
299	" Stella	Dau	1909	F
300	" Maude	Dau	1911	F
301	Childers, Clifford E	Son	1913	M
302	Chiltoskie, Will	Husb	1858	M
303	Chiltoskie, Charlotte	Wife	1889	F
304	" Wahdih	Son	1899	M
305	" James	Son	1907	M
306	Clay, Timpson	Wid	1873	M
307	Teesateeki, Arch	Son	1897	M
308	" Awee	Dau	1900	F
309	" Jonah	Son	1903	M
310	Clark, Lottie A	Wife	1869	F
311	Atttee, Frederick H	Son	1894	M
312	" Sophia F	Dau	1896	F
313	Climbingbear, Ollie	Wid	1855	F
314	" Deliskie	Son	1876	M
315	Cole, George Washington	Husb	1869	M

Roll Number		English Name	Relationship	Date of Birth	Sex
316	"	Walter	Son	1898	M
317	"	Jewel	Son	1900	M
318	"	John	Son	1904	M
319	"	Lula	Dau	1907	F
320	"	Wilford	Son	1909	M
321	"	Orna	Dau	1893	F
322	"	Ida	Dau	1890	F
323	"	William A	Husb	1879	M
324	"	Arley	Son	1905	M
325	"	Hollie	Son	1907	M
326	Cole, Ollie		Son	1909	M
327	"	Attla	Son	1910	M
328	"	Robert T	Husb	1887	M
329	"	Lloyd	Son	1912	M
330	"	George Emeryy[sic]	Son	1891	M
331	Coleman, Harrison E		Husb	1855	M
332	"	Birdie A	Dau	1896	F
333	"	Lucius Calvin	Son	1899	M
334	"	Nancy ME	Dau	1890	F
335	"	John N	Husb	1872	M
336	"	Julia N	Dau	1904	F
337	"	Henry J	Son	1906	M
338	"	Geo Washington	Husb	1879	M
339	"	Lillian M	Dau	1906	F
340	"	May Emaline	Dau	1909	F
341	"	Jesse James	Son	1906	M
342	"	William Edward	Husb	1881	M
343	"	Julius Roosevelt	Son	1904	M
344	"	Sarah Eliza	Dau	1906	F
345	"	Lillie M	Dau	1910	F
346	"	Wm Robert	Son	1912	M
347	"	Simon Peter	Husb	1884	M
348	"	Oscar	Son	1910	M
349	"	Otealve G	Dau	1911	F
350	"	Pearl May	Dau	1913	F
351	Conley, John		Wid	1861	M
352	"	Luke	Son	1896	M
353	"	John Jr	Son	1890	M
354	Conseen, Jack		Husb	1889	M
355	"	Eliza G	Wife	1893	F
356	"	Annie G	Dau	1913	F
357	"	Thompson	Husb	1891	M
358	"	Irene A	Wife	1874	F
359	Arch, Noah		St-Son	1895	M
360	"	Codeskie	St-Son	1899	M

North Carolina Eastern Cherokee Census 1915-1922
June 30,1915   Taken by: James E. Henderson
1915-1916   Volume I

Roll Number	English Name	Relationship	Date of Birth	Sex
361	" Winnie	St-Dau	1906	F
362	" Annie	St-Dau	1909	F
363	Conseen, Breast	Wid	1862	M
364	" Dahney	Dau	1896	F
365	" Willie	Son	1899	M
366	" James	Son	1888	M
367	" Jack	Wid	1836	M
368	" Peter	Husb	1879	M
369	" Nancy	Wife	1877	F
370	" Harry	Son	1905	M
371	" Joe	Son	1907	M
372	" Ida	Dau	1909	F
373	" John Ropetwister	Husb	1860	M
374	" Annie Arneach	Wife	1854	F
375	" Japson	Son	1910	M
376	Conseen, Kata	Dau	1864	F
377	" Martha	Dau	1898	F
378	Cook, Jessie Leora	Wife	1891	F
379	" Vernie Lee	Dau	1909	F
380	" Inez Gertrude	Dau	1911	F
381	" Randel Eggar	Son	1913	M
382	Cooper, Stavy Jane	Wife	1868	F
383	" Curtis	Son	1896	M
384	" Frankie	Dau	1897	F
385	" Leila	Dau	1898	F
386	" Fannie	Dau	1900	F
387	" Myrtle	Dau	1902	F
388	" Fred	Son	1905	M
389	" Selma	Dau	1908	F
390	" Mary Joe	Dau	1910	F
391	" Arnold	Son	1894	M
392	Rave, Martha Cornsilk	Wife	1886	F
393	" Morris Washing'n	Son	1913	M
394	" Wilmont Arnold	Son	1915	M
395	Cornsilk, John	Husb	1891	M
396	" Famous	Son	1912	M
397	" Armstrong	Husb	1852	M
398	" Annie	Wife	1859	F
399	" Hettie	Dau	1898	F
400	" Howard	Son	1900	M
401	Cornsilk, L Dow	Husb	1881	M
402	" Nancy	Wife	1882	F
403	" Woody	Son	1909	M
404	" Emma	Dau	1911	F
405	" Jacob	Son	1914	M

11

North Carolina Eastern Cherokee Census 1915-1922
June 30,1915   Taken by: James E. Henderson
1915-1916   Volume I

Roll Number	English Name	Relationship	Date of Birth	Sex
406	" York	Husb	1867	M
407	" Eann	Wife	1858	F
408	Saunooke, Jennie	Ward	1903	F
409	Harding, Mary Josephine Craig	Wife	1877	F
410	Craig, Robert Donley	Son	1905	M
411	Harding, Harold	Son	1912	M
412	" Florence S	Dau	1914	F
413	Craig, William W	Husb	1886	M
414	" Lillie V	Dau	1914	F
415	" Frank	Husb	1894	M
416	" Elvira H	Wife	1897	F
417	Crooks, Bessie Meroney	Wife	1881	F
418	Crow, Ute	Husb	1887	M
419	" Robert Henry	Son	1914	M
420	" Mary	Wife	1873	F
421	" Callie	Dau	1904	F
422	" Albert	Son	1906	M
423	" Lucy	Dau	1911	F
424	" Iva	Dau	1913	F
425	" Caroline	Wid	1837	F
426	Crow, Wesley R	Singl	1875	M
427	" Joseph	Husb	1869	M
428	" Annie	Wife	1865	F
429	" Boyd	Son	1895	M
430	" John Wesley	Husb	1889	M
431	" Mollie Endros	Wife	1878	F
432	" Joseph	Son	1911	M
433	" James David	Son	1914	M
434	Endros, Edwin	St-Son	1908	M
435	Crow, David	Husb	1889	M
436	" Sallie	Wife	1890	F
437	" Samuel	Son	1907	M
438	" Rachel	Dau	1908	F
439	" Stacy	Dau	1909	F
440	" Nancy	Dau	1911	F
441	" Aquaishoe	Son	1888	M
442	" Ossie	Hus	1883	M
443	Martha Toineeta	Wife	1889	F
444	" Dinah	Dau	1913	F
445	" Sevier	Husb	1860	M
446	" Dora	Dau	1896	F
447	" Arthur	Son	1899	M
448	" Luther	Son	1899	M
449	" Lossie	Son	1901	M
450	" Robert	Son	1894	M

Roll Number	English Name	Relationship	Date of Birth	Sex
451	Cucumber, Dorcas	Wid	1851	F
452	" Dakie	Dau	1897	F
453	" William	Son	1879	M
454	" Gena	Husb	1881	M
455	" Katie	Wife	1881	F
456	" Noah	Son	1883	M
457	" Squinchey	Son	1910	M
458	Saunooke, Ollie	St-Dau	1905	F
459	Cucumber, Arch	Husb	1888	M
460	" Ollie Youngbird	Wife	1868	F
461	Youngbird, James	St-Son	1900	M
462	" Walkinnih	St-Dau	1905	F
463	Cucumber, James	Husb	1894	M
464	" Lizzie Reed	Wife	1894	F
465	" Jennie	Dau	1911	F
466	" Mason	Son	1913	M
467	" Moses	Wid	1877	M
468	" John D	Son	1909	M
469	Dahnenolih or Smoke	Wid	1858	M
470	Dailey, Gita IR	Wife	1891	F
471	Davis, Wilste	Husb	1847	M
472	" Elsie	Wife	1853	F
473	" Joe	Husb	1873	M
474	" Katie	Wife	1858	F
475	" Quaitih	Wid	1837	F
476	Davis, Rebecca	Wife	1853	F
477	" Charley	Husb	1873	M
478	" Issac	Son	1899	M
479	" David	Son	1901	M
480	" George	Son	1905	M
481	" Callie	Dau	1909	F
482	" Israel	Son	1894	M
483	Deaver, Mary E Robersn	Wife	1874	F
484	" John Robert	Son	1909	M
485	Delegeskih, John	Wdor	1851	M
486	Taylor, James Deleges'h	Grd-Son	1903	M
487	Delegeskih, Alkinney	Son	1883	M
488	Taylor, Leander	Son	1906	M
489	" John	Son	1909	M
490	Dobson, John	Husb	1822	M
491	" Mary George	Wife	1860	F
492	George Kans	Grd-Son	1896	M
493	Littlejohn, Aggie	Ward	1895	F
494	Dockery, Emma J Payne	Wife	1882	F
495	" Elsie Arlena	Dau	1906	F

Roll Number		English Name	Relationship	Date of Birth	Sex
496	"	Ralph Burton	Son	1908	M
497	"	Cora P	Dau	1910	F
498	"	Dora Lee	Dau	1913	F
499	Donley, Robert L		Husb	1872	M
500	"	Sarah Eugenia	Dau	1914	F
501	Driver, Wesley		Husb	1872	M
502	"	Agnes	Wife	1870	F
503	"	John	Son	1899	M
504	"	Lucinda	Dau	1902	F
505	"	Sallie	Dau	1906	F
506	"	John Hill	Husb	1855	M
507	"	Sallie Calhoun	Wife	1837	F
508	"	Judas	Husb	1869	M
509	"	Eliza	Wife	1868	F
510	"	Annie	Div-Wife	1845	F
511	"	Jimmy	Husb	1839	M
512	"	Betty	Wife	1843	F
513	"	Russell B	Husb	1874	M
514	"	Marion	Dau	1904	F
515	"	Elsie	Dau	1907	F
516	"	Wesley	Son	1912	M
517	"	Goliath B	Husb	1876	M
518	"	Helen Ester	Dau	1909	F
519	"	Chekelelee	Husb	1884	M
520	"	Ollio	Wife	1886	F
521	"	Rosa	Dau	1902	F
522	"	George	Son	1904	M
523	"	Mason	Son	1909	M
524	"	Sag	Son	1913	M
525	"	Dickey	Husb	1850	M
526	Driver, Etta		Wife	1879	F
527	"	Nannie	Dau	1906	F
528	"	Dehart	Son	1909	M
529	"	John	Son	1912	M
530	"	William	Son	1873	M
531	"	Eliza	Dau	1871	F
532	"	Ned	Son	1897	M
533	"	Adam	Son	1901	M
534	Duncan, Lillian V		Wife	1877	F
535	"	Sybil	Dau	1906	F
536	Eubank, Lillie		Wife	1888	F
537	"	Joseph	Son	1906	M
538	"	Lillie M	Dau	1908	F
539	"	Verlin R	Son	1909	M
540	"	Clarence	Son	1911	M

Roll Number	English Name	Relationship	Date of Birth	Sex
541	Feather, Lawyer	Husb	1863	M
542	" Mary	Wife	1869	F
543	" Gahtayah	Dau	1900	F
544	" Jonah	Son	1906	M
545	Featherhead, Wilson	Husb	1876	M
546	" Nancy	Wife	1844	F
547	Finger, Sophronia C	Wife	1876	F
548	" Samuel A	Son	1898	M
549	" Leonia	Dau	1905	F
550	" Elmer Eugene	Son	1908	M
551	Finger, Ruby Irene	Dau	1911	F
552	Leo, Ramona G Finger	Wife	1896	F
553	Fox, Squirrel	Bach	1859	M
554	Fodder, Jennie	Widw	1842	F
555	Hornbuckle, Daniel	Grd-Son	1896	M
556	Fortner, Sis	Wife	1871	F
557	Foster, Alice	Wife	1876	F
558	" Elsie	Dau	1899	F
559	" Robert	Son	1901	M
560	" Burton	Son	1903	M
561	" Lee Roy	Son	1906	M
562	French, Linda Otter	Widw	1894	F
563	" Awee	Wife	1878	F
564	" Meroney	Son	1897	M
565	" Morgan	Son	1900	M
566	" Soggie	Son	1902	M
567	" George	Son	1905	M
568	" Jonah	Son	1907	M
569	" Lizzie	Dau	1909	F
570	" Wallie	Div-Wife	1880	F
571	" Ned	Son	1900	M
572	" Nellie	Dau	1902	F
573	" Katy	Dau	1907	F
574	" Jesse	Son	1905	M
575	Garland, Elizabeth	Widw	1830	F
576	Garland, Tullius B	Husb	1850	M
577	" John Basco	Husb	1879	M
578	" Frank	Son	1906	M
579	" Fred	Son	1908	M
580	" Edgar	Son	1911	M
581	" Roxianna	Dau	1858	F
582	" Elizabeth	Dau	1887	F
583	" William Sherman	Son	1866	M
584	" Jesse Lafayette	Husb	1856	M
585	" Emery	Son	1903	M

Roll Number		English Name	Relationship	Date of Birth	Sex
586	"	Radie Elmer	Dau	1906	F
587	"	Leonze	Husb	1885	M
588	"	Homelee	Son	1910	M
589	Teague, Jessie May Garland		Wife	1892	F
590	George, Dawson		Husb	1860	M
591	"	Mary	Wife	1859	F
592	"	Annie	Dau	1883	F
593	"	Manley	Son	1890	M
594	"	Davis	Husb	1851	M
595	"	Rosa E Biddix	Wife	1879	F
596	Biddix, Jennie		St-Dau	1903	F
597	"	Polly	St-Dau	1907	F
598	George, Shon		Bach	1871	M
599	"	Elijah	Husb	1874	M
600	"	Nicey Wilnotih	Wife	1887	F
601	Wilnoty, Aggy		St-Dau	1906	F
602	"	Nancy	St-Dau	1907	F
603	George, Lewis		Son	1904	M
604	"	Martha	Dau	1905	F
605	"	Cornelia	Dau	1907	F
606	"	Lettie	Dau	1911	F
607	"	Green	Sing	1909	M
608	"	Joe Stone	Husb	1857	M
609	"	Elizabeth	Wife	1859	F
610	"	Jacob	Husb	1897	M
611	"	Nola S	Wife	1897	F
612	"	Celia	Dau	1900	F
613	"	Jackson	Son	1903	M
614	"	Bessie Taylor	Wid	1897	F
615	"	Manda	Dau	1911	F
616	"	Esther	Wid	1856	F
617	"	Elijah	Bach	1877	M
618	"	Logan	Son	1888	M
619	"	Julia V	Wife	1875	F
620	"	Lottie V	Dau	1905	F
621	"	Wallace L	Son	1908	M
622	"	Shell	Bach	1860	M
623	Goin, Sally		Dau	1849	F
624	"	Bird Chopper	Husb	1869	M
625	"	Ollie	Wife	1872	F
626	Goin, Daniel		Son	1899	M
627	"	Emeline	Dau	1909	F
628	Goings, James		Widr	1832	F
629	Goings, Snake		Husb	1857	M
630	"	Nancy	Wife	1866	F

Roll Number	English Name	Relationship	Date of Birth	Sex
631	Greybeard, Lillie	Maid	1892	F
632	" Ezekiel	Bach	1840	M
633	" Aggie	Maid	1850	F
634	Green, Cora E Payne	Wife	1884	F
635	" Lurlie Beatrice	Dau	1907	F
636	" Bonnie Lee	Dau	1909	F
637	" Blanche J	Dau	1912	F
638	Griffin, Daisy Yonce	Wife	1892	F
639	" Nola	Dau	1911	F
640	" Ima	Dau	1913	F
641	Hawkins, Dora Parilee	Wife	1882	F
642	" Charlie Leonard	Son	1904	M
643	" Luther	Son	1909	M
644	" Delia May	Dau	1911	F
645	Hill, Soggy M	Husb	1881	M
646	" Henrietta	Wife	1874	F
647	" Maul	Div-Husb	1847	M
648	" Blain	Husb	1886	M
649	" Luzene	Wife	1883	F
650	" Sequohyeh,[sic] Ammons	St-Son	1905	M
651	Hill, Viola Nellie	Dau	1909	F
652	" Birdie Charlotte	Dau	1911	F
653	" Ned	Son	1888	M
654	" Levi	Husb	1890	M
655	" Laura Jane Wolfe	Wife	1890	F
656	" Lawrence	Son	1912	M
657	" Abraham	Husb	1864	M
658	" Annie	Wife	1872	F
659	" Hensley	Son	1899	M
660	" Callie	Dau	1902	F
661	Holland, Jennie	Wife	1886	F
662	" Grace	Dau	1904	F
663	" David	Son	1908	M
664	Hornbuckle, Rebecca	Widw	1848	F
665	" Maggie	Maid	1880	F
666	" Israel	Son	1908	M
667	" William	Husb	1882	M
668	" Jennie C	Wife	1886	F
669	" Clarence	Son	1910	M
670	" Nora	Dau	1912	F
671	" John Otter	Husb	1871	M
672	" Mattie	Wife	1865	F
673	" Dahnih	Dau	1905	F
674	" Caroline	Widr	1860	F
675	" John L	Husb	1884	M

North Carolina Eastern Cherokee Census 1915-1922
June 30,1915   Taken by: James E. Henderson
1915-1916   Volume I

Roll Number	English Name	Relationship	Date of Birth	Sex
676	Hornbuckle, Matrtha[sic]	Wife	1882	F
677	" Ben	Son	1913	M
678	" Jeff Davis	Widr	1864	M
679	" Jeff Davis Jr	Son	1892	M
680	" George	Husb	1877	M
681	" Melissa	Dau	1896	F
682	" Alice May	Dau	1898	F
683	" Hartman	Son	1901	M
684	" Olive Ann	Dau	1903	F
685	" John Russell	Son	1905	M
686	" William Allen	Son	1908	M
687	" Clifford	Son	1910	M
688	" Thurman	Son	1912	M
689	" William	Husb	1870	M
690	" Fred	Son	1896	M
691	" Dora	Dau	1899	F
692	" Wilson	Son	1901	M
693	" Maggie	Dau	1905	F
694	" Jennie	Dau	1911	F
695	Jack, Nancy	Didw[sic]	1837	F
696	Jackson, John	Husb	1836	M
697	" Stavy	Wife	1846	F
698	" Jack	Son	1892	M
699	" Lawyer	Husb	1873	M
700	" Dakie	Wife	1871	F
701	Jackson, Florence	Dau	1903	F
702	" Ella	Dau	1895	F
703	" Eliza	Wdw	1848	F
704	" Bob	Husb	1876	M
705	" Caroline	Wife	1880	F
706	" Wesley	Son	1900	M
707	" David	Son	1902	M
708	" Eddie	Son	1904	M
709	" Ikee	Son	1909	M
710	" Jacob	Husb	1894	F
711	Jessan, Lydia	Widw	1855	F
712	" Joseph	Son	1894	M
713	" Dahnola	Widr	1880	F
714	" Elnora	Dau	1909	F
715	" Lillian	Dau	1910	F
716	" John J Astor	Son	1913	M
717	Johnson, Jim	Son	1850	M
718	" Addison	Son	1886	M
719	" Yona	Husb	1880	M
720	" Dora	Wife	1884	F

Roll Number		English Name	Relationship	Date of Birth	Sex
721	"	Frank TR	Son	1909	M
722	"	Margaret G	Dau	1912	F
723	"	Jimpsie	Husb	1874	M
724	"	Ella	Wife	1858	F
725	"	Stephen	Husb	1846	M
726	Johnson, Jennie		Wife	1850	F
727	Jessan, Sim Dehart		Grd-Son	1904	M
728	Johnson, Taskigee		Husb	1878	M
729	"	Sally Oosowee	Wife	1878	F
730	Oosowee, Rachel		St-Dau	1897	F
731	"	Tahquette	St-Son	1899	M
732	Johnson, Jane (Jennie)		Widw	1889	F
733	"	Tom	Son	1909	M
734	"	Jonah	Son	1911	S
735	"	Tempa	Dau	1890	F
736	"	Isaac	Son	1893	M
737	Jumper, Ute		Husb	1873	M
738	"	Betsey	Wife	1874	F
739	"	Stansil	Son	1899	M
740	"	Edward	Son	1901	M
741	"	James U	Son	1904	M
742	"	Thomas	Son	1906	M
743	"	Henry	Son	1908	M
744	"	Ella	Dau	1909	F
745	"	Sarah	Dau	1913	F
746	Junaluskie, Jim		Son	1892	M
747	Jordan, William Clark		Husb	1848	M
748	"	Alfred	Son	1894	M
749	Hodges, Ollie Jordan		Wife	1895	F
750	Jordan, William H		Son	1888	M
751	Kalonaheskie, Esiah		Widr	1855	M
752	"	Martha	Dau	1902	F
753	"	Tom	Son	1888	M
754	"	Abram	Husb	1884	M
755	"	Charley	Son	1886	M
756	"	Joe	Son	1888	M
757	Keg, James		Husb	1842	M
758	"	Katy	Wife	1857	F
759	"	Matthew	Husb	1866	M
760	"	Rebecca	Dau	1910	F
761	"	Fannie	Dau	1914	F
762	"	Delia Ann	Wife	1891	F
763	"	William Harrison	Son	1910	M
764	"	Clarence Emerson	Son	1913	M
765	Kunteeskih		Husb	1850	M

Roll Number	English Name	Relationship	Date of Birth	Sex
766	" Sahwahchi	Wife	1846	F
767	Waidsutte, Bird	Nep	1910	M
768	Ladd, Bonney Rogers	Wife	1892	F
769	" Mark	Son	1911	M
770	Lambert, John N	Husb	1862	M
771	" Lloyd	Husb	1883	M
772	" Sallie	Wife	1880	F
773	" Luzene	St-Dau	1901	F
774	" Ollie	Dau	1905	F
775	" Nellie	Dau	1907	F
776	Lambert, Richard	Son	1909	M
777	" Ruth	Dau	1913	F
778	" Charley	Husb	1886	M
779	" Mary Arch	Wife	1887	F
780	" Jackson	Son	1906	M
781	" John Adams	Son	1911	M
782	" Luvenia	Dau	1915	F
783	" Hugh N	Husb	1882	M
784	" Alice Rosa	Wife	1884	F
785	" Paul LeRoy	Son	1909	M
786	" Arthur J	Son	1911	M
787	" Albert Smith	Son	1914	M
788	" Thomas B	Jusb[sic]	1874	M
789	" Nannie	Wife	1888	F
790	" Florence	Dau	1908	F
791	" Seymour	Son	1909	M
792	" Samuel C	Husb	1860	M
793	" Verdie	Dau	1895	F
794	" Corbett	Son	1897	M
795	" Cora Lee	Dau	1900	F
796	" Julia	Dau	1901	F
797	" Theodore	Son	1904	M
798	" Oney	Dau	1906	F
799	" Gaylord	Son	1909	M
800	" Lillian N	Dau	1912	F
801	Hipps, Nannie Lambert	Wife	1893	F
802	" Nina Marie	Dau	1913	F
803	Lambert, Claudie	Husb	1891	M
804	" Albert J	Husb	1852	M
805	" Jesse B	Husb	1877	M
806	" Minnie Stiles	Wife	1890	F
807	" Carl Glen	Son	1911	M
808	" Jessie Evelyn	Dau	191	F
809	" James W	Husb	1875	M
810	" Bessie	Dau	1900	F

Roll Number	English Name	Relationship	Date of Birth	Sex
811	" Hugh H	Son	1902	M
812	" Ida M	Dau	1909	F
813	" Lula P	Dau	19111[sic]	F
814	" Mintha A	Dau	1913	F
815	" Thomas O	Husb	1879	M
816	" Joseph C	Son	1903	M
816[sic]	" Henry H	Son	1904	M
818	" John A	Son	1906	M
819	" Sallie N	Dau	1909	F
820	" Nellie	Dau	1911	F
821	" Columbus	Husb	1870	M
822	" Harvey	Son	1897	M
823	" Carson	Son	1904	M
824	" Hugh J	Husb	1874	M
825	" Pearl B	Dau	1999[sic]	F
826	Lambert, Andrew J	Son	1901	M
827	" Isaac	Son	1903	M
828	" Dora	Dau	1908	F
829	" George	Son	1909	M
830	" Pearson	Ward	1899	M
831	" Ethel	Dau	1912	F
832	" Monroe	Husb	1857	M
833	" Jesse	Son	1895	M
834	" Fitzsimmons	Son	1897	M
835	" Flora	Gnd-Dau	1901	F
836	Maney, Minnie Araminta	Gnd-Dau	1905	F
837	" Ruth	Gnd-Dau	1907	F
838	" Bruce Garrett	Gnd-Son	1909	M
839	Lambert, Fred	Son	1895	M
840	" Charles	Son	1893	M
841	" Joseph Jackson	Husb	1895	M
842	" Cora Palestine	Dau	1906	F
843	" Leonard Carson	Son	1908	M
844	" Williard	Son	1910	M
845	" Gillian	Son	1912	M
846	" ? Baby	Dau	1915	F
847	" Edward Monroe	Son	1907	M
848	" Ed	Husb	1887	M
849	Larch, William	Son	1876	M
850	" David	Son	1883	M
851	Lee, Samuel	Husb	1890	M
852	" William Clyde	Son	1912	M
853	" Debrada	Dau	1899	F
854	" Edith	Dau	1896	F
855	" Alonzo	Husb	1874	M

Roll Number	English Name	Relationship	Date of Birth	Sex
856	" Alice May	Dau	1902	F
857	" Myrtle Gertrude	Dau	1907	F
858	Ledford, Sampson	Son	1885	M
859	" Charlie	Husb	1883	M
860	Maggie Walkingstick	Wife	1892	F
861	" Jake	Husb	1874	M
862	" Mary	Wife	1885	F
863	" Amy	Dau	1908	F
864	" Onih	Widw	1853	F
865	" Riley	Husb	1875	M
866	" Polly	Wife	1882	F
867	" Joe	Son	1901	M
868	" Kina	Dau	1903	F
869	" Caroline	Dau	1907	F
870	" Willie	Son	1909	M
871	" Caroline MR	Wife	1884	F
872	" Minnie	Dau	1896	F
873	" Cora	Dau	1903	F
874	" Adkins	Son	1906	M
875	" Charles, Alvin	Son	1908	M
876	Ledford, Bonnie Marie	Dau	1910	F
877	" Cyrus Atlas	Son	1912	M
878	" Iowa	Dau	1894	F
879	Lefevers, Temoxzenah G	Wife	1881	F
880	" Linnie	Dau	1900	F
881	" William	Son	1901	M
882	Littlejohn, Saunooke	Husb	1863	M
883	" Ann Eliza	Wife	1868	F
884	" Henson	Son	1899	M
885	" John	Son	1902	M
886	" Owen	Son	1906	M
887	" Addie	Dau	1908	F
888	" Emeline	Dau	1909	F
889	" Wiggins	Husb	1891	M
890	" Caroiline[sic] S	Wife	1888	F
891	Standingdeer, Sallie A	St-Dau	1909	F
892	Littlejohn, Edward J	Son	1913	M
893	" Will	Div-Husb	1868	M
894	" Guy	Son	1897	M
895	" Katie	Dau	1898	F
896	" Isaac	Son	1900	M
897	" Elowih	Husb	1875	M
898	" Annie	Wife	1879	F
899	" Sallie Ann	Dau	1902	F
900	" Sherman	Son	1904	M

North Carolina Eastern Cherokee Census 1915-1922
June 30,1915   Taken by: James E. Henderson
1915-1916   Volume I

Roll Number	English Name	Relationship	Date of Birth	Sex
901	Littlejohn, Jefferson	Son	1907	M
902	" Wesley	Son	1909	M
903	" Lizzie	Dau	1913	F
904	Tooni, Rachel	Ward	1899	F
905	Littlejohn, Minda	Dau	1912	F
906	George, Goolarche	Ward	1902	M
907	Littlejohn, Ropetwister	Husb	1865	M
908	" Annie	Wife	1877	F
909	Wilnoty, Joseph	St-Son	1895	M
910	" Ned	" Son	1896	M
911	Littlejohn, Sallie	Dau	1903	F
912	" Isaac	Son	1906	M
913	" Eugene	Son	1912	M
914	" Bessie	Dau	1914	F
915	" Goliath	Husb	1870	M
916	Locust, John	Husb	1852	M
917	" Polly Ann	Wife	1856	F
918	" Noah	Husb	1882	M
919	" Lewis	Son	1901	M
920	" Laura B	Dau	1903	F
921	" Tiney	Dau	1905	F
922	" Martha	Dau	1910	F
923	" Homer	Son	1911	M
924	" Josephine	Dau	1913	F
925	Long, Adam	Husb	1847	M
926	Long, Polly	Wife	1856	F
927	" Eve	Dau	1898	F
928	" Nola	Dau	1901	F
929	" Joe	Husb	1858	M
930	" Nancy George	Wife	1839	F
931	" Charley	Son	1894	M
932	" Peter	Husb	1879	M
933	" Anona C	Wife	1890	F
934	Harris, Rachel Long	Wife	1883	F
935	Long, Dobson	Husb	1858	M
936	" Sallie	Wife	1870	F
937	" William Gaffney	Son	1897	M
938	" Elizabeth	Dau	1901	F
939	" Johnson	Husb	1862	M
940	" Maggie	Wife	1876	F
941	" Annie	Dau	1907	F
942	" Scott	Husb	1852	M
943	" Sallie	Wife	1862	F
944	Davis, Anita	St-Dau	1897	F
945	" Emeline	" "	1900	F

North Carolina Eastern Cherokee Census 1915-1922
June 30,1915   Taken by: James E. Henderson
1915-1916   Volume I

Roll Number	English Name	Relationship	Date of Birth	Sex
946	Long, Agginy	Dau	1905	F
947	" John	Husb	1873	M
948	" Eve	Wife	1865	F
949	" Rachel	Dau	1874	F
950	" Joseph Bigwitch	Husb	1882	M
951	Long, Sallie	Wife	1879	F
952	Crow, Alice	Stp-Dau	1897	F
953	Long, Lucy	Dau	1905	F
954	" Etta	Dau	1907	F
955	" Lloyd	Son	1909	M
956	" John	Son	1911	M
957	" Nellie	Widow	1844	F
958	" Charlie Bigwitch	Son	1888	M
959	" Jackson	Husb	1855	M
960	" Sallie	Widow	1877	F
961	" Long Bear	Son	1898	M
962	" Lucy	Dau	1900	F
963	" Aggie	Dau	1902	F
964	" Bettie	Dau	1904	F
965	" Isaac	Son	1906	M
966	" Lena	Dau	1908	F
967	" Martha	Dau	1913	F
968	" Will West	Husb	1871	M
969	" Annie Welch	Wife	1891	F
970	Lossih, John Dehart	Husb	1870	M
971	" Laura	Wife	1870	F
972	" John Jr	Son	1898	M
973	" Jesse James	Son	1907	M
974	" Jonas	Son	------	M
975	" Lizzie	Dau	1891	F
976	Lossih, Henry	Husb	1871	M
977	" Aggie	Wife	1880	F
978	" Rosa	Dau	1907	F
979	" Cowell	Son	1909	M
980	" Abel	Son	1911	M
981	" Mary	Dau	1913	F
982	Ross, McKinley	St-Son	1901	M
983	Loissh, Jonas	Husb	1873	M
984	" Nicey	Wife	1880	F
985	Walkingstick, Tom	Ward	1908	M
986	Lossih, Jennie	Widw	1858	F
987	" Dom	Son	1896	M
988	" Candy	Son	1898	M
989	" John R	Son	1903	M
990	" Hayes	Son	1905	M

Roll Number	English Name	Relationship	Date of Birth	Sex
991	" David	Son	1893	M
992	" Leander	Son	1885	M
993	Loudermilk, Josephine G	Wife	1877	F
994	" Nora	Dau	1902	F
995	" Elmer	Son	1902	M
996	" Cora	Dau	1906	F
997	" Clinton	Son	1908	M
998	" Cynthia Ann	Wife	1861	F
999	" Rebecca	Dau	1899	F
1000	" John R	Husb	1879	M
1001	Loudermilk, Luther	Son	1900	M
1002	" William R	Son	1904	M
1003	" Julia	Dau	1906	F
1004	" Lee Roy	Son	1909	M
1005	" Willford Thurston	Son	1913	M
1006	Bowen, John B	Bach	1861	M
1007	" John	Husb	1861	M
1008	" Sis	Wife	1862	F
1009	Kalonuheskie, Nannie	St-Dau	1897	F
1010	Maney, Eve	Wife	1896	F
1011	" Mary	Dau	1904	F
1012	" John	Son	1906	M
1013	" Allen Jacob	Son	1908	M
1014	" Alice	Dau	1910	F
1015	" Caroline	Dau	1913	F
1016	Martin, Suate	Wder	1856	M
1017	" Thomas	Son	1887	M
1018	" George	Husb	1861	M
1019	" Lucy	Wife	1872	F
1020	" Charles	Son	1908	M
1021	" Wesley	Husb	1895	M
1022	" Margaret Smoker	Wife	1896	F
1023	Mashburn, Harriet A	Wife	1878	F
1024	Littlejohn, Mindy (Old #2187)	Dau	1894	F
1025	Murphy, Manco (Old #2188)	Dau	1891	F
1026	Mashburn, Frank	Son[sic]	1900	M
1027	" Bessie	Dau	1901	F
1028	" James L	Son	1904	M
1029	" Sarah	Dau	1906	F
1030	" Thomas	Son	1911	F
1031	" Leora R	Wife	1884	F
1032	" Minnie	Dau	1902	F
1033	" Mattie	Dau	1904	F

North Carolina Eastern Cherokee Census 1915-1922
June 30,1915   Taken by: James E. Henderson
1915-1916   Volume I

Roll Number	English Name	Relationship	Date of Birth	Sex
1034	" Bertha	Dau	1907	F
1035	" Ninia	Dau	1908	F
1036	Matthews, Lillian WL	Wife	1881	F
1037	" Eva Addie	Dau	1905	F
1038	" Gradie R	Son	1908	M
1039	" Mary Laurena	Dau	1911	F
1040	McAllister, Harriet AG	Wife	1866	F
1041	McCoy, David	Husb	1873	M
1042	" Marinda	Dau	1900	F
1043	" James	Son	1902	M
1044	" Julia	Dau	1904	F
1045	" Stella	Dau	1906	F
1046	" Jesse	Son	1910	M
1047	" Bessie	Dau	1911	F
1048	" Eva	Dau	1913	F
1049	" John	Husb	1875	M
1050	" Pearson	Son	1897	M
1051	McCoy, Mary	Dau	1901	F
1052	" James	Son	1905	M
1053	" Walter	Son	1909	M
1054	" James	Husb	1881	M
1055	" William T	Son	1905	M
1056	" Jose h H[sic]	Son	1907	M
1057	" Frank	Son	1912	M
1058	McLeymore, John L	Husb	1854	M
1059	" Cora May	Dau	1905	F
1060	" Samuel H	Husb	1855	M
1061	" Morrell	Son	1901	M
1062	" Samuel Ross	Son	1906	M
1063	" Elsie Bonni	Dau	1909	F
1064	" William Glenn	Son	1910	M
1065	" Kimmit E	Son	1913	M
1066	Meroney, Martha Ann	Widow	1835	F
1067	" John G	Husb	1865	M
1068	" Sallie Belle	Dau	1895	F
1069	" Mays	Dau	1897	F
1070	" Gertrude	Dau	1899	F
1071	" Bailey B	Son	1901	M
1072	" Dellax[sic]	Dau	1906	F
1073	Youngbird, Rufus	Son	1887	M
1074	" Soggie	Son	1890	----
	Should follow#2200			
1075	" Yohnih	Dau	1892	F
1076	Taylor, Lula Meroney	Wife	1890	F
1077	Meroney, Fred	Son	1906	M

Roll Number	English Name	Relationship	Date of Birth	Sex
1078	" Bailey Barton	Husb	1866	M
1079	" Margaret A	Dau	1899	F
1080	" Richard B	Son	1902	M
1081	" Felix P	Son	1904	M
1082	" William H	Son	1877	M
1083	" Raymond	Son	1913	M
1084	Miller, Flourney Rogers	Wife	1889	F
1085	" Vessey	Dau	1908	F
1086	" Bessie	Dau	1909	F
1087	" Vertie	Dau	1911	F
1088	Monroe, Nora A	Wife	1880	F
1089	" Charles A	Son	1907	M
1090	" Hugh N	Son	1910	M
1091	Mumblehead, John D	Husb	1864	M
1092	" Dahney	Wife	1881	F
1093	" Roger L	Son	1896	M
1094	" Elizabeth	Dau	1906	F
1095	" James B	Son	1889	M
1096	" James W	Son	1880	M
1097	Murphy, Martin	Husb	1835	M
1098	" Fred	Son	1907	M
1099	" Howard	Son	1894	M
1100	" Louisa	Wife	1886	F
1101	Murphy, Margaret	Dau	1888	F
1102	" Isabella	Dau	1890	F
1103	" Jesse	Husb	1863	M
1104	" Mary McC	Wife	1877	F
1105	" Lillian Arch	Cousin of Wife	1905	F
1106	" William	Husb	1890	M
1107	" Lafayette	Son	1910	M
1108	" Robert	Son	1912	M
1109	" David	Husb	1830	M
1110	" Joseph Marion	Husb	1854	M
1111	" Cinthia Minerva	Dau	1895	F
1112	" Clifford	Grd-Son	1904	M
1113	Garrett, Lillie AM	Wife	1880	F
1114	" Alger	Son	1908	M
1115	" Hollie	Dau	1909	F
1116	" Allen	Son	1912	M
1117	" Mary J	Dau	1881	F
1118	Patterson, Eustice JM	Wife	1885	F
1119	" Bob	Son	1905	M
1120	" Mae	Dau	1906	F
1121	Stroud, Flora BM Mur-	Wife	1887	F
1122	" Dessie	Dau	1909	F

North Carolina Eastern Cherokee Census 1915-1922
June 30,1915   Taken by: James E. Henderson
1915-1916   Volume I

Roll Number	English Name	Relationship	Date of Birth	Sex
1123	" Ethel	Dau	1912	F
1124	Murphy, Lloyd C	Son	1892	M
1125	" Henry L	Husb	1878	M
1126	Murphy, Edgar	Son	1901	M
1127	" Rayburn	Son	1903	M
1128	" Maud	Dau	1905	F
1129	" Verdie B	Dau	1909	F
1130	Okwataga, Elizabeth	Widow	1831	F
1131	Oocumma, James	Widower	1854	M
1132	" Annie	Dau	1895	F
1133	" Wilson	Husb	1878	M
1134	" Enoch	Son	1889	M
1135	" Alex	Husb	1866	M
1136	" Annie	Wife	1889	F
1137	" Fannie	Dau	1909	F
1138	" John	Son	1912	M
1139	Ned, Ezekiel	Husb	1862	M
1140	" Susan	Wife	1862	F
1141	Nick, Chiltoskie	Son	1882	M
1142	Notty Tom, Peter	Husb	1869	M
1143	" Nancy	Wife	1882	F
1144	Oosowee, John Jr	Husb	1877	M
1145	" Sally Conseen	Wife	1871	F
1146	Conseen, Buck	St-Son	1906	M
1147	Oosowee, Samuel Davis	Husb	1872	M
1148	" Susie	Wife	1877	F
1149	Otter, Andrew	Husb	1871	M
1150	" Sarah	Wife	1866	F
1151	Otter, Jackson	Son	1899	M
1152	" Matilda	Dau	1901	F
1153	" Ollie	Dau	1903	F
1154	" Allen	Husb	1879	M
1155	" Winnie	Wife	1876	F
1156	" Sallie	Dau	1901	F
1157	" Ollie	Widow	1850	F
1158	Owl, Sokiney	Son	1889	M
1159	" Dinah	Wife	1861	F
1160	" Enoch	Son	1899	M
1161	" Betsy	Dau	1905	F
1162	" William	Son	1893	M
1163	" Jonah	Husb	1882	M
11 64	" Julia	Wife	1891	F
1165	" Philip	Son	1909	M
1166	" Ellie	Son	1913	M
1167	" Ammons	Husb	1890	M

Roll Number		English Name	Relationship	Date of Birth	Sex
1168	"	Lizzie E	Wife	1889	F
1169	"	Gertrude E	Dau	1914	F
1170	"	George	Son	1895	M
1171	"	Henry	Son	1897	M
1172	"	Frell	Son	1899	M
1173	"	Thomas	Son	1905	M
1174	"	Charlotte	Dau	1909	F
1175	"	David	Son	1894	M
1176	Owl, Lula		Dau	1892	F
1177	"	John	Husb	1859	M
1178	"	Margaret	Dau	1904	F
1179	"	Annie Nicey	Dau	1906	F
1180	"	Lewis	Son	1910	M
1181	"	Sampson	Husb	1854	M
1182	"	Agnes	Ward	1895	F
1183	"	Johnson	Husb	1878	M
1184	"	Stacy	Wife	1878	F
1185	"	Ernest	Son	1910	M
1186	"	Joseph	Son	1913	M
1187	"	Adam	Husb	1860	M
1188	"	Cornelia	Wife	1857	F
1189	"	Samuel	Son	1897	M
1190	"	David	Son	1897	M
1191	"	Martha	Dau	1900	F
1192	"	Quincey	Son	1905	M
1193	"	William	Husb	1884	M
1194	"	Thomas	Husb	1887	M
1195	"	Moses	Husb	1889	M
1196	Wolfe, John R		St-Son	1904	M
1197	"	William H	" "	1906	M
1198	"	Richard C	" "	1908	M
1199	Owl, Joseph Adam		Son	1914	M
1200	"	John	Son	1892	M
1201	Owl, James		Husb	1887	M
1202	"	Lloyd	Son	1909	M
1203	"	Stephenson	Son	1911	M
1204	"	Charlotte	Wife	1894	F
1205	"	Allen	Husb	1888	M
1206	"	Solomon	Husb	1864	M
1207	"	Alfred Bryson	Son	1897	M
1208	"	Lloyd S	Son	1900	M
1209	"	Cornelius	Son	1902	M
1210	"	Ethel	Dau	1906	F
1211	"	William David	Son	1907	M
1212	"	Dewitt	Son	1909	M

North Carolina Eastern Cherokee Census 1915-1922
June 30,1915   Taken by: James E. Henderson
1915-1916   Volume I

Roll Number	English Name	Relationship	Date of Birth	Sex
1213	" Edward	Son	1910	M
1214	" Martha Jane	Dau	1895	F
1215	" Theodore	Husb	1886	M
1216	Moody, Callie Owl	Wife	1888	F
1217	" Harlan	Dau	1914	F
1218	Owl, Mark	Husb	1892	M
1219	" Belvia S	Wife	1892	F
1220	" Jarrett	Son	1911	M
1221	" Oscar	Son	1912	M
1222	" Ralph	Son	1915	M
1223	Palmer, Dora Owl	Wife	1890	F
1224	" Linford	Son	1912	M
1225	" Haddington Davis	Son	1913	M
1226	Panther, Job	Husb	1884	M
1227	" Bettie	Wife	1858	F
1228	" Mark	Husb	1875	M
1229	" Windy Littlejohn	Wife	1888	F
1230	" Simeon	Son	1913	M
1231	" Anna	Div-Wife	1863	F
1232	Partridge, Bird	Husb	1879	M
1233	" Elsie	Wife	1874	F
1234	George, Elmo Don	St-Son	1903	M
1235	Partridge, Sarah	Dau	1910	F
1236	" John	Son	1911	M
1237	" Winnie	Dau	1886	F
1238	French, Juanita MP	Dau	1909	F
1239	" Coleman B	Son	1912	M
1240	Partridge, Moses	Husb	1881	M
1241	" Sallie	Wife	1888	F
1242	" Savannah	Dau	1907	F
1243	" Sarah	Dau	1911	F
1244	" Jonas	Son	1914	M
1245	Parris, Catherine Cole	Wife	1884	F
1246	" Laura May	Dau	1907	F
1247	" Lola	Dau	1912	F
1248	Passamore, Nancy Jane	Wife	1878	F
1249	" Thomas M	Son	1902	M
1250	" Charles Alonzo	Son	1903	M
1251	Passamore, Rose Cordelia	Dau	1905	F
1252	" Oscar	Son	1907	M
1253	" David	Son	1912	M
1254	Patterson, Lula	Wife	1879	F
1255	" Oldham	Son	1902	M
1256	" Almer	Son	1907	M
1257	" Alwain	Son	1910	M

Roll Number	English Name	Relationship	Date of Birth	Sex
1258	" Ella Cole	Wife	1877	F
1259	" Alonzo	Son	1896	M
1260	" Ethel	Dau	1898	F
1261	" Elizabeth	Dau	1900	F
1262	" Celia	Dau	1902	F
1263	" Hobart	Son	1904	M
1264	" Arvil	Son	1906	M
1265	" Beadie	Dau	1908	F
1266	" Kenneth	Son	1909	M
1267	" Zida	Dau	1911	F
1268	Payne, Thomas	Husb	1845	M
1269	" Oliver Clem	Son	1892	M
1270	" William E	Husb	1872	M
1271	" Paly E	Son	1896	M
1272	" William Alfred	Son	1904	M
1273	" Lydia M	Dau	1906	F
1274	" Cynthia	Dau	1908	F
1275	" Gertrude	Dau	1910	F
1276	Payne, James M	Husb	1877	M
1277	" Rollin T	Son	1898	M
1278	" Albert F	Son	1900	M
1279	" Grace Lee	Dau	1904	F
1280	" Erma	Dau	1908	F
1281	" Carra	Dau	1910	F
1282	" Margie Eunice	Dau	1913	F
1283	Peckerwood, John	Husb	1848	M
1284	" Rebecca	Wife	1863	F
1285	" Lucy Ann	Widow	1858	F
1286	" McKinley	Son	1902	M
1287	Pheasant, John	Husb	1853	M
1288	" William	Husb	1883	M
1289	" Rachel Emma	Wife	1892	F
1290	" Jacob	Son	1911	M
1291	" Dora Jane	Dau	1891	F
1292	Porter, Florence	Widow	1863	F
1293	" Dewitt	Husb	1890	M
1294	" Iris	Dau	1892	F
1295	Powell, Dooga	Widow	1870	F
1296	" Sarah	Dau	1899	F
1297	" Holmes	Son	1902	M
1298	" Winnie	Dau	1905	F
1299	" Noah	Son	1908	M
1300	" Moses	Husb	1887	M
1301	Powell, Elkiny	Wife	1883	F
1302	" Stacy	Dau	1909	F

North Carolina Eastern Cherokee Census 1915-1922
June 30,1915   Taken by: James E. Henderson
1915-1916   Volume I

Roll Number		English Name	Relationship	Date of Birth	Sex
1303	"	Stansill	Son	1891	M
1304	"	John Alvin	Husb	1853	M
1305	Queen, Levi		Husb	1871	M
1306	"	Mary	Wife	1880	F
1307	"	Minda	Dau	1896	F
1308	"	Abraham	Son	1900	M
1309	"	Addie	Dau	1902	F
1310	"	Melinda	Dau	1905	F
1311	"	Lottie	Dau	1907	F
1312	"	Dinah	Dau	1909	F
1313	"	Lillie	Dau	1912	F
1314	"	Simpson	Husb	1873	M
1315	"	Olliney	Dau	1899	F
1316	"	Sallie	Wife	1881	F
1317	"	Nolen	Son	1901	M
1318	"	Mary	Dau	1903	F
1319	"	Bessie	Dau	1905	F
1320	"	John	Son	1907	M
1321	"	Rachel	Dau	1909	F
1322	"	Lucy	Dau	1912	F
1323	"	Jasper	Son	1895	M
1324	Raper, Alexander		Husb	1846	M
1325	"	William Thomas	Husb	1868	M
1326	Raper, Edgar		Son	1895	M
1327	"	Verdie	Dau	1897	F
1328	"	Daffney	Dau	1898	F
1329	"	Augustus	Son	1903	M
1330	"	James Curley	Son	1904	M
1331	"	William Arthur	Son	1908	M
1332	"	Bertha May	Dau	1910	F
1333	"	Windell Efton	Son	1912	M
1334	"	Jesse Lafayette	Husb	1871	M
1335	"	Cly Victor	Son	1898	M
1336	"	Claude Emery	Son	1899	M
1337	"	Curley Clinton	Dau	1901	F
1338	"	Minnie Corrine	Dau	1907	F
1339	"	William Cecil	Son	1913	M
1340	"	Marshall	Husb	1878	M
1341	"	Clarence Alwain	Son	1989[sic]	M
1342	"	Clinton	Son	1902	M
1343	"	Eva	Dau	1904	F
1344	"	Bonnie Bell	Dau	1907	F
1345	"	William Taft	Son	1909	M
1346	"	Rosa Ella	Dau	1911	F
1347	"	Martie Alexander	Husb	1893	M

Roll Number	English Name	Relationship	Date of Birth	Sex
1348	Mull, Effie Leora Raper	Wife	1894	F
1349	Raper, Charlie B	Husb	1876	M
1350	" Denver Lee	Son	1898	M
1351	Raper, Delta Clifford	Dau	1900	F
1352	" Pearl	Dau	1905	F
1353	" Homer W	Son	1911	M
1354	" Henry John	Husb	1881	M
1355	" Viola Ellen	Dau	1903	F
1356	" Ivan	Son	1905	M
1357	" Delia	Dau	1908	F
1358	" Iril	Son	1911	M
1359	" Thomas Martin	Husb	1856	M
1360	" James	Son	1896	M
1361	" Lizzie	Dau	1898	F
1362	" Julia	Dau	1900	F
1363	" Clifton	Son	1907	M
1364	" Lula	Dau	1909	F
1365	" Whoola B	Son	1888	M
1366	" Martin T	Son	1888	M
1367	" William B	Husb	1880	M
1368	" William	Son	1911	M
1369	" Lon	Husb	1881	M
1370	" Edna	Dau	1910	F
1371	" Gano	Widower	1883	M
1372	Ratley, Lucy	Div-Wife	1852	F
1373	Ratler, George W	Husb	1873	M
1374	" Polly	Wife	1873	F
1375	" Rachel	Dau	1896	F
1376	Ratler, Henson	Son	1898	M
1377	" Morgan	Son	1900	M
1378	" Mindah	Dau	1903	F
1379	" Bessie	Dau	1909	F
1380	" Ammons	Son	1911	M
1381	" John	Husb	1887	M
1382	" Emeline	Wife	1886	F
1383	" John West	Son	1907	M
1384	" Lucy	Dau	1909	F
1385	" Willie	Son	1911	M
1386	" Nancy	Widow	1855	F
1387	" Jonah	Son	1889	M
1388	" Robert	Son	1901	M
1389	" Walter	Son	1904	M
1390	Ratliff, William	Husb	1873	M
1391	" Elizabeth	Wife	1876	F
1392	" Emma	Dau	1902	F

Roll Number	English Name	Relationship	Date of Birth	Sex
1393	" Jacob	Son	1904	M
1394	" Ella	Dau	1907	F
1395	" Jonah	Son	1910	M
1396	" Myrtle M	Dau	1913	F
1397	" Lawyer	Bach	1880	M
1398	" James	Husb	1848	M
1399	Reagan, Hester Lambert	Wife	1889	F
1400	" Earnest	Son	1908	M
1401	Reagan, Polena	Dau	1910	F
1402	" Pollard	Son	1912	M
1403	Reed, James	Bach	1854	M
1404	" Rachel	Widow	1850	F
1405	" Minda	Grd-Dau	1895	F
1406	" Fiddell	Husb	1875	M
1407	" Addie H Lee	Wife	1893	F
1408	Lee, Josie	St-Dau	1910	F
1409	Reed, David	Bach	1861	M
1410	" Peter	Widower	1852	M
1411	" Cindy	Grd-Dau	1897	F
1412	" Jimmie	Son	1888	M
1413	" Lloyd	Son	1888	M
1414	" William	Husb	1884	M
1415	" Katie K	Wife	1891	F
1416	" Jackson	Son	1909	M
1417	" Cornelia	Dau	1911	F
1418	" Adam	Husb	1878	M
1419	" Sarah	Wife	1884	F
1420	" Rachel	Div-Wife	1884	F
1421	" Johnson	Son	1905	M
1422	" Samuel	Son	1911	M
1423	" Deweese	Div-Husb	1880	M
1424	" Nannie	Div-Wife	1884	F
1425	" Susanne	Dau	1905	F
1426	Reed, Sarah	Dau	1912	F
1427	" Maggie	Wife	1850	F
1428	" James W	Husb	1868	M
1429	" Agnes	Dau	1906	F
1430	" Willie Elmer	Son	1910	M
1431	" Meekerson	Son	1911	M
1432	George, Maggie G Reed	Wife	1888	F
1433	Richards, Mamie Payne	Wife	1887	F
1434	" Ruby Kate	Dau	1907	F
1435	" Willard Frances	Son	1909	M
1436	" Grace Lara	Dau	1912	F
1437	Riley, James	Son	1901	M

Roll Number	English Name	Relationship	Date of Birth	Sex
1438	Roberson, Iowa Isabella	Wife	1889	F
1439	" Etta	Dau	1908	F
1440	" AJ	Son	1911	M
1441	" Edward E	Husb	1877	M
1442	" Charlie Hobart	Son	1905	M
1443	" Howard Geoffrey	Son	1908	M
1444	" Henry H	Son	1910	M
1445	" Alvin W	Son	1912	M
1446	" Willie O	Son	1880	M
1447	" Thomas L	Husb	1883	M
1448	" William R	Son	1904	M
1449	" Harley T	Son	1908	M
1450	" Sarah Edith	Dau	1911	F
1451	Roberts, Lottie Smith	Wife	1877	F
1452	" Callie	Dau	1902	F
1453	" Walter	Son	1904	M
1454	" Fred	Son	1907	M
1455	" Lula	Dau	1907	F
1456	" Edna	Dau	1912	F
1457	Robinson, Ellen Raper	Wife	1865	F
1458	" Emeline	Dau	1897	F
1459	" Hadley	Son	1899	M
1460	Beavers, Fannie R	Wife	1894	F
1461	Rogers, Jeanette RP	Widow	1847	F
1462	" Martha Caroline	Wife	1870	F
1463	" William	Husb	1864	M
1464	" Oscar	Son	1896	M
1465	" Villa	Dau	1899	F
1466	" Floyd	Son	1902	M
1467	" Aster	Son	1905	M
1468	" Inez	Dau	1907	F
1469	Ropetwister, Manley	Son	1858	M
1470	Rose, Florence	Wife	1872	F
1471	" Jake	Son	1896	M
1472	" Grace	Dau	1900	F
1473	" Nora	"	1902	F
1474	" Cora	Dau	1905	F
1475	" Benjamin	Son	1908	M
1476	Rose, Thurman	Son	1910	M
1477	" Wayne	Son	1913	M
1478	" William	Son	1893	M
1479	Morgan, Bonnie Rose	Wife	1891	F
1480	" Agnes	Dau	1912	F
1481	Runningwolf	Husb	1879	M
1482	" " Mollie	Wife	1881	F

Roll Number	English Name	Relationship	Date of Birth	Sex
1483	" Lloyd	Son	1899	M
1484	" Ammons	Son	1904	M
1485	" Sallie	Dau	1907	F
1486	" Callie	Dau	1911	F
1487	" Wm McKinley	Son	1913	M
1488	Sampson, James	Husb	1853	M
1489	" Sallie	Wife	1863	F
1490	Cucumber, Arch	Ward	1905	M
1491	Sanders, Cudge Ellis	Husb	1861	M
1492	" Polly	Wife	1857	F
1493	" Moses	Son	1896	M
1494	Twin, Viola	Grd-Dau	1910	F
1495	Saunooke, Nancy	Widow	1852	F
1496	" Jim	Son	1889	M
1497	" Sally	Widow	1878	F
1498	" Kane	Son	1908	M
1499	" Essiek	Son	1912	M
1500	" William	Husb	1870	M
1501	Saunooke, Edward	Son	1900	M
1502	" Anderson	Son	1904	M
1503	" Osler	Son	1906	M
1504	" Oowanah	Son	1909	M
1505	" Friedman	Son	1911	M
1506	" Nettie	Dau	1913	F
1507	" Cora	Dau	1915	F
1508	" Joseph	Husb	1872	M
1509	" Margaret	Wife	1887	F
1510	" Emma	Dau	1910	F
1511	" Charles Logan	Son	1913	M
1512	" Nicodemus B	Son	1912	M
1513	" Stillwell	Widower	1842	M
1514	" Cindy	Dau	1899	F
1515	" Lillie	Dau	1906	F
1516	" Emeneeta	Son	1894	M
1517	" Malinda	Dau	1886	F
1518	" Nan	Dau	1890	F
1519	" Samuel	Husb	1879	M
1520	Ward, Rachel Saunooke	Wife	1886	F
1521	" Priscilla	Dau	1910	F
1522	Saunooke, Stillwell	Son	1891	M
1523	" Jackson	Son	1883	M
1524	Sauve, Minnie E Nick	Wife	1881	F
1525	" Marie Mabel	Dau	1908	F
1526	Sauve, Josephine E	Dau	1909	F
1527	" Joseph Peter	Son	1911	M

Roll Number	English Name	Relationship	Date of Birth	Sex
1528	Sawyer, Kiney	Div-Wife	1884	F
1529	" Thomas	Son	1906	M
1530	" Allen	Div-Husb	1877	M
1531	Screamer, James	Husb	1858	M
1532	" Cindy	Wife	1882	F
1533	" David	Husb	1891	M
1534	" Elnora F	Wife	1897	F
1535	" Soggy	Son	1894	M
1536	" Manus	Husb	1882	M
1537	" Nannie	Wife	1877	F
1538	" Kane	Son	1892	M
1539	" Enos	Div-Husb	1866	M
1540	Sequohyeh,[sic] Zachariah	Husb	1859	M
1541	" Louisa H	Wife	1861	F
1542	" Susan	Dau	1901	F
1543	" Alice	Dau	1903	F
1544	Hill, Minda	St-Dau	1898	F
1545	Sequohyeh,[sic] Noah J	Son	1885	M
1546	Sequohyeh[sic]	Widower	1847	M
1547	Shake-Ear, Fidella	Husb	1871	M
1548	" Sallie	Wife	1864	M
1549	Shell, John	Husb	1852	M
1550	" Sallie	Wife	1860	F
1551	Feather, Hettie	Ward	1897	F
1552	Shell, Ute	Husb	1878	M
1553	" Mattie	Wife	1885	F
1554	" Joseph	Son	1902	M
1555	" Joshua	Son	1908	M
1556	" Boyd	Son	1911	M
1557	Sherrill, John	Husb	1875	M
1558	" Mollie	Wife	1879	F
1559	Tramper, Kiney	St-Dau	1899	F
1560	Sherrill, Solemn	Son	1902	M
1561	" Julia	Dau	1906	F
1562	" Samuel	Son	1909	M
1563	" Andy	Son	1913	M
1564	Shuler, Georgia Craig	Widow	1884	F
1565	Simpson, Martha Owl	Wife	1877	F
1566	Skitty, Sevier	Son	1848	M
1567	Smith, Jacob L	Husb	1879	M
1568	" Olive	Wife	1879	F
1569	" Lawrence	Son	1907	M
1570	" Charles H	Son	1911	M
1571	" Mary Malvina	Wife	1862	F
1572	" Oliver	Son	1896	M

North Carolina Eastern Cherokee Census 1915-1922
June 30,1915   Taken by: James E. Henderson
1915-1916   Volume I

Roll Number		English Name	Relationship	Date of Birth	Sex
1573	"	James David	Husb	1878	M
1574	"	Lawrence	Son	1913	M
1575	"	Bertha B	Dau	1915	F
1576	Smith, Duffy		Son	1880	M
1577	"	Francis Elwood	Husb	1886	M
1578	"	Bettie Welch	Wife	1881	F
1579	"	Victor C	Son	1911	M
1580	"	Edgar A	Son	1914	M
1581	"	Clifford	Son	1914	M
1582	Maney, Charity Smith		Wife	1891	F
1583	"	Richard David	Son	1912	M
1584	"	James Oliver	Son	1913	M
1585	Smith, Noah		Husb	1883	M
1586	"	Earl H	Son	1907	M
1587	"	Ella A	Dau	1909	F
1588	"	Grace Rose	Dau	1911	F
1589	"	Martha Ann	Widow	1837	F
1590	"	Lewis H	Husb	1846	M
1591	"	Nancy	Wife	1851	F
1592	"	Rose B	Husb	1840	M
1593	"	Cynthia	Wife	1852	F
1594	"	Samuel A	Husb	1866	M
1595	"	Goldman	Son	1896	M
1596	"	David McKinley	Son	1901	M
1597	"	Jess	"	1903	M
1598	"	Margaret	Dau	1911	F
1599	"	Morten	Son	1913	M
1600	"	William Blain	Husb	1888	M
1601	Smith, Lucy Ann Davis		Wife	1891	F
1602	"	Annie	Dau	1911	F
1603	"	Joseph M	Son	1890	M
1604	"	Lorena M	Widow	1864	F
1605	"	Thaddeus Sibbald	Husb	1870	M
1606	"	Hartman	Son	1898	M
1607	"	Mary	Dau	1900	F
1608	"	Grace	Dau	1906	F
1609	"	Mildred	Dau	1910	F
1610	"	Helen	Dau	1913	F
1611	"	Carrie Elliott	Dau	1915	F
1612	"	Lloyd H	Husb	1873	M
1613	"	Roberson	Son	1901	M
1614	"	Elizabeth	Dau	1902	F
1615	"	Noah	Son	1904	M
1616	"	Tennie	Dau	1906	F
1617	"	John D	Son	1907	M

North Carolina Eastern Cherokee Census 1915-1922
June 30,1915   Taken by: James E. Henderson
1915-1916   Volume I

Roll Number	English Name	Relationship	Date of Birth	Sex
1618	" Duffy	Son	1910	M
1619	" Jarrett Jackson	Son	1913	M
1620	" George Lewis	Son	1879	M
1621	" Henry	Husb	1849	M
1622	" Russel	Son	1905	M
1623	" Hettie	Dau	1907	F
1624	" Myrtle	Dau	1909	F
1625	Rogers, Wesley Crow	St-Son	1901	M
1626	Rogers, Bessie	Dau	1912	F
1627	" Maggie	Dau	1893	F
1628	Smith, Roxie	Dau	1884	F
1629	" Thomas	Husb	1882	M
1630	" Buford Roy	Son	1909	M
1631	" Leaina	Dau	1911	F
1632	" Hosea Gilbert	Son	1913	M
1633	" John GA	Husb	1870	M
1634	" Josephine	Dau	1896	F
1635	" Rosena	Dau	1899	F
1636	" Bessie	Dau	1902	F
1637	" Robert S	Son	1904	M
1638	" Ross B	Son	1908	M
1639	" James CW	Son	1894	M
1640	" Velmer	Dau	1914	F
1641	Smoker, Aggie	Widow	1875	F
1642	" Willie	Son	1899	M
1643	" Peter	Son	1902	M
1644	" Charles	Son	1906	M
1645	" James	Husb	1890	M
1646	" Luzene Washington	Wife	1894	F
1647	" Davison	Son	1912	M
1648	" Will Sawyer	Husb	1871	M
1649	" Alkinney	Wife	1878	F
1650	" Moses	Son	1897	M
1651	Smoker, Awee	Dau	1897	F
1652	" Hunter	Son	1902	M
1653	" Lizzie	Dau	1905	F
1654	" Lucy	Dau	1907	F
1655	" Martha	Dau	1909	F
1656	" Hute	Son	1912	M
1657	" Samuel	Husb	1882	M
1658	" Stacy	Wife	1883	F
1659	" Bascom	Son	1903	M
1660	" Ollie	Dau	1905	F
1661	" Cornelia	Dau	1907	F
1662	" Bettie	Dau	1909	F

Roll Number	English Name	Relationship	Date of Birth	Sex
1663	" Caroline	Dau	1911	F
1664	" Lloyd	Husb	1871	M
1665	" Nancy	Wife	1858	F
1666	Sneed, William Sherman	Husb	1862	M
1667	" Samuel (White Wife)	Husb	1857	M
1668	" Mary C (White Husb)	Wife	1897	F
1669	Taylor, Inez Katherine	Dau	1914	F
1670	Sneed, Annie L	Dau	1898	F
1671	" Maude E	Dau	1900	F
1672	" John H	Husb	1853	M
1673	" Manco	Husb	1887	M
1674	" Sherman	Son	1912	M
1675	" Lawrence S	Son	1912	M
1676	Sneed, Osco	Husb	1879	M
1677	" Thomas Mack	Son	1907	M
1678	" William Harley	Son	1909	M
1679	" Alma	Dau	1910	F
1680	" James E	Son	1912	M
1681	" Campbell	Husb	1888	M
1682	" Mindy	Wife	1890	F
1683	" Carrie	Dau	1909	F
1684	" Ernest	Son	1910	M
1685	" Pocahontas	Dau	1911	F
1686	" Claudie May	Dau	1915	F
1687	" Peco	Husb	1875	M
1688	" Sarah	Dau	1901	F
1689	" Blakely	Son	1905	M
1690	" Stella	Dau	1908	F
1691	" Lillian K	Dau	1910	F
1692	" Woodrow	Son	1913	M
1693	Salolaneeta, Bird	Husb	1842	M
1694	" Leander	Husb	1865	M
1695	" Annie	Wife	1879	F
1696	Kalonuheskie, Edith	Niece of Wife	1909	F
1697	Salolaneeta, Linda	Maid	1865	F
1698	Souther, Dora Cole	Wife	1887	F
1699	" Delpha	Son	1909	M
1700	" Hartford	Son	1910	M
1701	Spray, Gertrude Henrian-	Dau	1887	F
1702	Squirrel, George	Husb	1864	M
1703	" Rebecca	Wife	1875	F
1704	" Sequechee	Son	1900	M
1705	" Mary	Dau	1903	F
1706	" Nancy	Widow	1880	F
1707	" Kimsey	Son	1897	M

North Carolina Eastern Cherokee Census 1915-1922
June 30,1915   Taken by: James E. Henderson
1915-1916   Volume I

Roll Number	English Name	Relationship	Date of Birth	Sex
1708	" Dora	Dau	1899	F
1709	" Dinah	Dau	1901	F
1710	" Daniel	Son	1904	M
1711	" Ollie	Dau	1906	F
1712	" Shepherd	Son	1908	M
1713	" Abel	Son	1910	M
1714	" David	Son	1914	M
1715	Standingdeer, Nancy	Widow	1851	F
1716	" Lowen	Son	1883	M
1717	" Wesley	Husb	1857	M
1718	" Nancy	Wife	1863	F
1719	" Junaluska R	Husb	1882	M
1720	" Carl	Husb	1882	M
1721	" Mary Smith	Wife	1884	F
1722	" Cecelia	Dau	1907	F
1723	" Virginia	Dau	1909	F
1724	" Roxanna	Dau	1911	F
1725	" Mary	Dau	1913	F
1726	Standingdeer, Andy	Husb	1859	M
1727	" Margaret	Wife	1859	F
1728	Standingwater, Alexander	Widower	1857	M
1729	Stamper, Ned	Husb	1869	M
1730	" Sallie Ann	Wife	1876	F
1731	" Nettie	Dau	1897	F
1732	" Caroline	Dau	1899	F
1733	" William	Son	1901	M
1734	" Lizzie	Dau	1903	F
1735	" Sarah	Dau	1907	F
1736	" Emma	Dau	1909	F
1737	" Roberson	Son	1913	M
1738	Stiles, Mary E Payne	Wife	1870	F
1739	" Oliver	Son	1898	M
1740	" Clem	Son	1904	M
1741	" Hal	Son	1906	M
1742	" Gilbert	Son	1894	M
1743	Burrell, Emma Stiles	Wife	1896	F
1744	Stiles, Theodocia EP	Wife	1880	F
1745	" Rufus Virgil	Son	1900	M
1746	" Thomas Luster	Son	1898	M
1747	" Cora Alma	Dau	1902	F
1748	" Lloyd	Son	1905	M
1749	" Ella	Dau	1907	F
1750	" Wilfred	Son	1909	M
1751	Stiles, Hallie l	Wife	1888	F
1752	" Floyd	Son	1910	M

North Carolina Eastern Cherokee Census 1915-1922
June 30,1915   Taken by: James E. Henderson
1915-1916   Volume I

Roll Number	English Name	Relationship	Date of Birth	Sex
1753	" Sadie Lee	Dau	1912	F
1754	St Jermain, Nicey I	Wife	1871	F
1755	Suagih, Anna	Widow	1854	F
1756	"	Husb	1840	M
1757	" Mary	Wife	1855	F
1758	Sutaga, Sallie	Grd-Dau	1905	F
1759	Swayney, Laura J	Wife	1858	F
1760	" Luzene	Dau	1899	F
1761	" Calcina	Dau	1894	F
1762	" Jess W	Div-Husb	1888	M
1763	" Lorenzo Dow	Husb	1878	M
1764	" Amanda	Dau	1902	F
1765	" Frank D	Son	1905	M
1766	" Shurman A	Son	1908	M
1767	" Grace	Dau	1910	F
1768	" Dora N	Dau	1912	F
1769	" John Wesley	Husb	1883	M
1770	" Alvin Walker	Son	1910	M
1771	" Laura Josephine	Dau	1912	F
1772	Swimmer, Mary	Widow	1859	F
1773	" John	Husb	1877	M
1774	" Lucy Ann	Wife	1884	F
1775	" Obediah	Son	1906	M
1776	Swimmer, Grace	Dau	1908	F
1777	" Luke	Son	1909	M
1778	" George	Son	1911	M
1779	" Runaway	Husb	1878	M
1780	" Annie	Wife	1883	F
1781	Conley, Linda	Half Sister of Wife	1904	F
1782	Swimmer, Thomas	Husb	1855	M
1783	" Annie	Wife	1859	F
1784	Tahquette, John	Div-Husb	1856	M
1785	" Martha	Maid	1864	F
1786	" John Alfred	Husb	1870	M
1787	" Anna Elizabeth	Wife	1874	F
1788	" Emily	Dau	1906	F
1789	" Frank Glenn	Son	1907	M
1790	" Howard Wayne	Son	1909	M
1791	" Amy Elizabeth	Dau	1910	F
1792	" Marion	Dau	1910	F
1793	" Alfred	Son[sic]	1913	M
1794	" ? (Baby)	Son	1915	M
1795	Tail, Jim	Son	1841	M
1796	Tailor, Eliza	Widow	1857	F
1797	" Julius	Son	1899	M

42

North Carolina Eastern Cherokee Census 1915-1922
June 30, 1915   Taken by: James E. Henderson
1915-1916   Volume I

Roll Number	English Name	Relationship	Date of Birth	Sex
1798	" Timpson	Son	1900	M
1799	" David	Son	1902	M
1800	" William	Son	1907	M
1801	Taylor, Jack	Husb	1890	M
1802	" Rebecca A	Wife	1896	F
1803	" Sallie	Widow	1841	F
1804	" Julius	Husb	1878	M
1805	" Stacy	Wife	1875	F
1806	" Sherman	Husb	1882	M
1807	" Maggie	Wife	1887	F
1808	" Alkinney	Dau	1905	F
1809	" George	Son	1909	M
1810	" Eva	Dau	1911	F
1811	" Largie	Son	1914	M
1812	" Jesse	Husb	1866	M
1813	" Stacy	Wife	1861	F
1814	" John	Husb	1891	M
1815	" Nannie Welch	Wife	1894	F
1816	" Eva	Dau	1912	F
1817	" Seymore	Son	1914	M
1818	Teesateskee, John	Husb	1860	M
1819	" Jennie	Wife	1860	F
1820	" Welch	Son	1896	M
1821	" Lloyd	Son	1900	M
1822	Teesateski, Sampson	Husb	1891	M
1823	" Annie George	Wife	1895	F
1824	" Sallie	Dau	1912	F
1825	" Jesse	Husb	1887	M
1826	Teeesateski, Polly Bird	Wife	1884	F
1827	Bird, Bettie	St-Dau	1901	F
1828	" Solomon	" Son	1903	M
1829	" Lucy Ann	" Dau	1907	F
1830	" Adam	" Son	1910	M
1831	Teesateski, Sarah	Dau	1912	F
1832	" Will	Husb	1853	M
1833	" Nessih	Wife	1855	F
1834	Ledford, Allen	Ward	1905	M
1835	Teesateskie, Steve	Ward	1906	M
1836	" Josie	Ward	1908	F
1837	" Illinois	Husb	1875	M
1838	" Cindy Smoker	Wife	1888	F
1839	Teesateski, Noah	Husb	1885	M
1840	" Ella	Wife	1886	F
1841	" Willie	Son	1907	M
1842	" George	Son	1910	M

North Carolina Eastern Cherokee Census 1915-1922
June 30, 1915   Taken by: James E. Henderson
1915-1916   Volume I

Roll Number	English Name	Relationship	Date of Birth	Sex
1843	Teleskie, Ezekiel	Widower	1853	M
1844	" Jesse	Husb	1891	M
1845	" Sallie Littlej'n	Wife	1880	F
1846	Littlejohn, Garrett	St-Son	1906	M
1847	Tootale, Nancy	Dau	1825[sic]	F
1848	Tewatley, Rose	Wife	1850	F
1849	" Kane	Son	1886	M
1850	" William	Son	1875	M
1851	Tewatley, Adam	Husb	1875	M
1852	" Desdemonia Crow	Wife	1897	F
1853	Thompson, Enos	Widower	1861	M
1854	" Goliath	Son	1898	M
1855	" Peter	Son	1887	M
1856	" Johnson	Husb	1866	M
1857	" Nancy	Wife	1868	F
1858	" David	Son	1897	M
1859	" James W	Son	1900	M
1860	" Jonanni	Son	1903	M
1861	" Annie	Dau	1906	F
1862	" Simon	Son	1894	M
1863	" Jackson	Son	1905	M
1864	" Ahsinnih	Husb	1884	M
1865	" Sallie Welch	Wife	1879	F
1866	" Mary W	Wife	1876	F
1867	" Iowa	Dau	1895	F
1868	" Olin	Son	1897	M
1869	" Greeley	Son	1899	M
1870	" Verdie	Dau	1903	F
1871	" Iris	Dau	1905	F
1872	" Lawrence	Son	1909	M
1873	" Willard	Son	1911	M
1874	" Wilson	Husb	1888	M
1875	" Rebecca	Wife	1890	F
1876	Thompson, Elizabeth	Dau	1913	F
1877	" Martha W	Widow	1874	F
1878	" William H	Son	1895	M
1879	" Mata	Dau	1897	F
1880	" Minnie	Dau	1899	F
1881	" Elbert	Son	1900	M
1882	" Braska L	Dau	1902	F
1883	" Atha W	Dau	1903	F
1884	" Jewel	Son	1905	M
1885	" Marvin	Son	1906	M
1886	" Walter	Son	1908	M
1887	Thomas, Rhoda RC	Wife	1866	F

44

Roll Number	English Name	Relationship	Date of Birth	Sex
1888	" Ella Henrietta	Dau	1906	F
1889	" William Harrison	Son	1908	M
1890	" Lula CE	Dau	1909	F
1891	" James Henry	Son	1911	M
1892	" Andrew Roosevelt	Son	1913	M
1893	" Dallas J	Son	1914	M
1894	" Allison M	Son	1914	M
1895	" Berdie J	Dau	1915	F
1896	Timpson, James	Husb	1853	M
1897	Coleman, Timpson Callie	Wife	1893	F
1898	" Leslie	Husb	------	M
1899	" Ida Evelin	Dau	1913	F
1900	Timpson, John S	Husb	1885	M
1901	Timpson, Vestry	Dau	1913	F
1902	" Columbus H	Husb	1889	M
1903	" James Q	Husb	1881	M
1904	" Lawrence Arthur	Son	1909	M
1905	" Lexie May	Dau	1911	F
1906	" Humphrey P	Son	1858	M
1907	Toe, Johnson	Husb	1857	M
1908	Saunooke, Nannie	Grd-Dau	1898	F
1909	" Polly	Grd-Dau	1906	F
1910	Toe, Campbell	Son	1870	M
1911	Toineeta, Loney	Husb	1860	M
1912	" Sallie	Wife	1860	F
1913	" Caroline	Dau	1895	F
1914	Lossie, Solomon	Ward	1899	M
1915	Toineeta, West	Son	1882	M
1916	" George	Husb	1883	M
1917	Welch, Lloyd	St-Son	1895	M
1918	" Theodore A	" "	1897	M
1919	" Clarence	" "	1899	M
1920	" Richard R	" "	1903	M
1921	Toineeta, Edwin T	Son	1909	M
1922	" F Geneva	Dau	1911	F
1923	" Janet	Dau	1913	F
1924	" Nick	Husb	1868	M
1925	" Bettie	Wife	1881	F
1926	Toineeta, Arneach	Son	1893	M
1927	" Suagih	Son	1889	M
1928	Tollie, Lizzie	Wife	1887	F
1929	Tooni, Squinchey	Husb	1840	M
1930	" Lydia	Wife	1856	F
1931	" Moses	Son	1889	M
1932	" Mike	Husb	1874	M

North Carolina Eastern Cherokee Census 1915-1922
June 30,1915   Taken by: James E. Henderson
1915-1916   Volume I

Roll Number	English Name	Relationship	Date of Birth	Sex
1933	" Anna	Wife	1876	F
1934	" Elijah	Son	1900	M
1935	" Nancy	Dau	1903	F
1936	" Lizzie	Dau	1911	F
1937	" Joseph	Widower	1856	M
1938	" Andy	Son	1892	M
1939	" Nicey	Dau	1886	F
1940	" Jukius	Husb	1876	M
1941	" Lizzie	Wife	1882	F
1942	" Rachel	Dau	1909	F
1943	" Lossel	Son	1910	M
1944	" John	Son	1915	M
1945	" Nancy	Wife	1879	F
1946	" Nannie	Dau	1903	F
1947	" Isaac	Son	1905	M
1948	" Mary	Dau	1899	F
1949	" Wannie	Dau	1909	F
1950	" Ollie	Dau	1913	F
1951	Tramper, Chiltoskie	Son	1881	M
1952	" Amineeta	Son	1890	M
1953	" Lottie	Dau	1894	F
1954	Ute, Mary	Wife	1842	F
1955	Wachacha, Roxie	Widow	1861	F
1956	" Susie	Dau	1896	F
1957	" John Wayne	Son	1898	M
1958	" Jesse	Son	1900	M
1959	" Winnie	Dau	1901	F
1960	" Oney	Dau	1904	F
1961	" John C	Son	1893	M
1962	" Nancy	Dau	1893	F
1963	" Posey	Son	1894	M
1964	" Nessie	Dau	1881	F
1965	" Jarrett	Husb	1874	M
1966	" Amanda Teesats'k	Wife	1895	F
1967	" ? (?)	Son	1913	M
1968	" James	Son	1886	M
1969	" Sarah	Dau	1889	F
1970	" Char[sic] Charles	Husb	1890	M
1971	Wahyahnetah, John	Husb	1843	M
1972	" Awee	Wife	1853	F
1973	" Posey	Grd-Son	1900	M
1974	" Sampson	Son	1883	M
1975	" Allen	Husb	1874	M
1976	Wahyahnetah, Sallie	Wife	1869	F
1977	" William	Husb	1870	M

North Carolina Eastern Cherokee Census 1915-1922
June 30,1915   Taken by: James E. Henderson
1915-1916   Volume I

Roll Number	English Name	Relationship	Date of Birth	Sex
1978	" Kamie	Wife	1877	F
1979	" Maggie	Dau	1901	F
1980	" Samuel	Son	1904	M
1981	" LeRoy	Son	1907	M
1982	" Bertha	Dau	1909	F
1983	" Ethel	Dau	1911	F
1984	" Robert Austin	Son	1913	M
1985	Waidsutte, Bird	Husb	1877	M
1986	" Mary	Wife	1870	F
1987	Axe, Manda	St-Dau	1899	F
1988	Waidsutte, Lee	Son	1903	M
1989	Axe, Peter	Son	1893	M
1990	Waidsutte, Davis	Husb	1872	M
1991	" Nancy	Wife	1876	F
1992	" Addison	Son	1910	M
1993	" Ben	Husb	1862	M
1994	" Kiney	Wife	1882	F
1995	" Margaret	Dau	1912	F
1996	Walkingstick, Mike	Husb	1845	M
1997	" Caroline	Wife	1856	F
1998	" James	Husb	1885	M
1999	" Lucy Ann	Wife	1883	F
2000	Jasper	Husb	1872	M
2001	Walkingstick, Annie	Wife	1883	F
2002	" Mason	Son	1903	M
2003	" Willie	Son	1907	M
2004	" Maggie	Dau	1905	F
2005	" Adam	Son	1909	M
2006	" John	Son	1911	M
2007	" John	Husn[sic]	1850	M
2008	" Walsa	Wife	1871	F
2009	" Moses	Son	1894	M
2010	" Mike	Son	1902	M
2011	" Enoch	Son	1909	M
2012	" Ollie Maud	Dau	1912	F
2013	" Owen	Husb	1889	M
2014	" Linda	Wife	1884	F
2015	" Cinda	Dau	1909	F
2016	" Lizzie	Dau	1911	F
2017	" Bascom	Son	1889	M
2018	Wallace, James	Husb	1878	M
2019	" Tahquette Owl	Son	1903	M
2020	Warlick, Edna May	Dau	1900	F
2021	Ramsey, Roxie	Dau	1909	F
2022	Watty, Goolarche	Husb	1877	M

North Carolina Eastern Cherokee Census 1915-1922
June 30,1915   Taken by: James E. Henderson
1915-1916   Volume I

Roll Number		English Name	Relationship	Date of Birth	Sex
2023	"	Nesssih	Wife	1876	F
2024	"	Stephen	Son	1897	M
2025	"	Kiney	Dau	1900	F
2026	Watty, Lizzie		Dau	1902	F
2027	"	Polly	Dau	1906	F
2028	"	Olsie	Dau	1909	F
2029	"	[sic]	Husb	1835	M
2030	"	Uhnahyih	Wife	1843	F
2031	"	Ute	Husb	1865	M
2032	"	Mary	Wife	1871	F
2033	Washington, Key		Div-Husb	1853	M
2034	"	Elizabeth	Widow	1840	F
2035	"	Joseph	Husb	1882	M
2036	"	Stella B	Wife	1885	F
2037	"	Richard B	Son	1910	M
2038	"	Josephine	Dau	1913	F
2039	"	Jesse	Husb	1875	M
2040	"	Ollie	Wife	1875	F
2041	Reed, Luzene		St-Dau	1897	F
2042	Washington, Amy		Dau	1905	F
2043	"	George	Son	1907	M
2044	"	Jonas	Son	1910	M
2045	Wayne, John		Husb	1862	M
2046	"	Jennie	Wife	1870	F
2047	"	Will John	Husb	1874	M
2048	"	Yehkinnie	Dau	1911	F
2049	Webster, Rachel A		Widow	1842	F
2050	"	William Lawrence	Husb	1872	M
2051	Webster, Jetter Columbus		Son	1897	M
2052	"	Carrie	Dau	1900	F
2053	"	Norma	Dau	1903	F
2054	"	William Robert	Son	1906	M
2055	"	William Lewis	Son	1912	M
2056	Welch, John C		Widower	1844	M
2057	"	Lucinda C	Dau	1893	F
2058	"	Mark G	Son	1877	M
2059	"	Lottie	Dau	1887	F
2060	"	Willie	Husb	1891	M
2061	"	Maude F	Wife	1894	F
2062	"	William Elliott	Son	1915	M
2063	"	Jimmy	Son	1891	M
2064	"	Lotty	Wife	1891	F
2065	"	Elizabeth Regina	Dau	1913	F
2066	"	John	Son	1894	M
2067	"	Edward R	Son	1903	M

North Carolina Eastern Cherokee Census 1915-1922
June 30,1915   Taken by: James E. Henderson
1915-1916   Volume I

Roll Number	English Name	Relationship	Date of Birth	Sex
2068	" Nannie H	Dau	1905	F
2069	" Mary	Dau	1892	F
2070	" James B	Sep-Husb	1873	M
2071	" Sampson	Husb	1858	M
2072	" Lizzie	Wife	1865	F
2073	" Epheus	Husb	1883	M
2074	" Stacy	Wife	1890	F
2075	" Juna	Son	1908	M
2076	Welch, Martha	Dau	1911	F
2077	" Edward	Husb	1885	M
2078	" David	Son	1911	M
2079	" Lydia T	Wife	1891	F
2080	" Lucy	Dau	1914	F
2081	" Nannie	Widow	1862	F
2082	" Lucinda	Dau	1883	F
2083	" Moses	Son	1886	M
2084	" Davis	Husb	1868	M
2085	" Ned	Son	1904	M
2086	" Lizzie	Dau	1906	F
2087	" Jennie	Dau	1909	F
2088	" Jesse	Son	1893	M
2089	" Martha Wolfe	Wife	1889	F
2090	" Calinah	Dau	1913	F
2091	" James	Son	1892	M
2092	" Lizzie Bell	Dau	1914	F
2093	" Elijah	Husb	1862	M
2094	" Ann Eliza	Wife	1859	F
2095	Armachain, Jonah	St-Son	1895	M
2096	Welch, Mark	Son	1900	M
2097	" Ollie	Dau	1903	F
2098	" James Elijah	Son	1889	M
2099	" Adam	Husb	1886	M
2100	" Ann Eliza	Wife	1891	F
2101	Welch, Frank Churchill	Son	1908	M
2102	" Russell	Son	1911	M
2103	" Charlotte	Dau	1913	F
2104	" Corneeta	Husb	1880	M
2105	" Nancy Hill	Wife	1892	F
2106	" Charles Davis	Son	1913	M
2107	Wesley, Judas	Husb	1876	M
2108	" Jennie	Wife	1858	F
2109	Lowen, John	St-Son	1895	M
2110	Whippoorwill, Manley	Son	1884	M
2111	Wildcat	Widower	1856	M
2112	" Daniel	Husb	1881	M

Roll Number	English Name	Relationship	Date of Birth	Sex
2113	" Elsie	Wife	1866	F
2114	Will, John	Husb	1862	M
2115	" Jane	Wife	1872	F
2116	" James	Son	1903	M
2117	" Alice	Dau	1905	F
2118	" David	Son	1907	M
2119	" Luzene	Dau	1909	F
2120	" Nellie	Dau	1912	F
2121	Wilnothi, Simon	Husb	1891	M
2122	" Amanda Tewatley	Wife	1890	F
2123	" Lot	Widower	1850	M
2124	Wilnoty, Ned	Husb	1851	M
2125	" Sally	Wife	1852	F
2126	Wilnoty, Mink	Son	1845	M
2127	" Moses	Husb	1881	M
2128	" Julius	Son	1909	M
2129	" Elizabeth	Dau	1914	F
2130	Greybeard, James	St-Son	1901	M
2131	" Sallie	" Dau	1898	F
2132	Macon, Katherine W	Wife	1886	F
2133	Wolfe, Edward	Husb	1891	M
2134	" Standingturkey	Husb	1869	M
2135	" Callie	Wife	1873	F
2136	" William Johnson	Husb	1877	M
2137	" Martha	Wife	1873	F
2138	" Joe	Son	1902	M
2139	" Addison	Son	1906	M
2140	" Lilly	Dau	1909	F
2141	" Eli	Son	1911	M
2142	" Susan	Widow	1851	F
2143	" Ward	Husb	1890	M
2144	" Caroline W	Wife	1899	F
2145	" John Lossie	Husb	1863	M
2146	" Nancy Lossie	Wife	1855	F
2147	" Dawson	Husb	1891	M
2148	" Diannah	Dau	1914	F
2149	" Lloyd Lossie	Son	1899	M
2150	" Jacob	Husb	1871	M
2151	Wolfe, Nelcina	Wife	1873	F
2152	" Joseph	Son	1897	M
2153	" Jesse	Son	1900	M
2154	" Alice	Dau	1907	F
2155	" Lucinda	Dau	1910	F
2156	" Abel	Son	1903	M
2157	" Jacob Jake	Son	1913	M

North Carolina Eastern Cherokee Census 1915-1922
June 30,1915   Taken by: James E. Henderson
1915-1916   Volume I

Roll Number	English Name	Relationship	Date of Birth	Sex
2158	" John W	Husb	1870	M
2159	" Linda	Wife	1873	F
2160	" Walker	Son	1905	M
2161	" Salkiny	Dau	1910	F
2162	" Jogohe	Dau	1913	F
2163	" Junaluska	Son	1884	M
2164	" Owen	Husb	1884	M
2165	" Susie Armachain	Wife	1859	F
2166	" Taqua	Husb	1889	M
2167	" Ancie F	Wife	1898	F
2168	" Alice	Dau	1912	F
2169	" Moses	Husb	1847	M
2170	" Jane	Wife	1861	F
2171	" Jonah	Son	1894	M
2172	" Joseph H	Husb	1872	M
2173	" Jennie	Wife	1870	F
2174	" Callie	Dau	1898	F
2175	" Polly	Dau	1846	F
2176	Wolfe, Mary Elizabeth	Dau	1884	F
2177	Wolfe, James T	Husb	1887	M
2178	" Bettie Smoke	Wife	1895	F
2179	" William W	Son	1912	M
2180	" Edwin Wendall	Son	1914	M
2181	" Pearle Margaret	Dau	1888	F
2182	Kalonuheskie, Josephine	Niece	1916	F
2183	Wolfe, Amanda Wakie	Dau	1890	F
2184	" Charles Hicks	Son	1892	M
2185	" George Lloyd	Sep-Husb	1877	M
2186	" Jessie May	Dau	1909	F
2187	" Charles Ray	Son	1910	M
2188	" David	Husb	1843	M
2189	" Louis Henry	Husb	1872	M
2190	" Isabella	Dau	1896	F
2191	" Amanda Jane	Dau	1899	F
2192	" Elaza Pauline	Dau	1903	F
2193	" James William	Son	1906	M
2194	" Frederick S	Son	1909	M
2195	" Dessie Cleo	Dau	1913	F
2196	" Louis David	Son	1892	M
2197	" Jowan	Husb	1848	M
2198	" Sallie	Wife	1860	F
2199	Yonce, Nancy S	Wife	1852	F
2200	Youngbird, Wesley	Son	1894	M
2201	Youngdeer, John	Husb	1856	M
2202	" Betsy	Wife	1853	F

Roll Number		English Name	Relationship	Date of Birth	Sex
2203	"	Martha	Dau	1896	F
2204	"	Moody	Son	1899	M
2205	"	Eli	Son	1881	M
2206	"	Jonah	Son	1883	M
2207	"	Jesse	Son	1887	M
2208	"	Stephen	Son	1889	M
2209	"	Jacob	Husb	1872	M
2210	"	Lunsih	Wife	1853	F
2211	Coleman, Valley		Dau	1915	F

```
Males 21 years of age and over------------      555
Males under 21 years of age---------------      627
Females 18 years of age and over---------      509
Females under 18 years of age-------------      520
              Total-----------------------------     2211
```

```
Total Males-------     1182
Total Females----     1029
     Total--------     2211
```

5-1142

DEPARTMENT OF THE INTERIOR

UNITED STATES INDIAN SERVICE

Transmits
Census Roll
Eastern Band
Cherokees

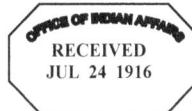

OFFICE OF INDIAN AFFAIRS
RECEIVED
JUL 24 1916

Cherokee Indian School,
Cherokee, NC   July 26, 1916

The Commissioner of Indian Affairs
          Washington, DC

     Sir:

     I am inclosing herewith census roll of the Eastern Band of Cherokee Indians for
the years ending June 30, 1916

                    Very respectfully,
                         James E Henderson
                              Superintendent

CENSUS ROLL

of

EASTERN BAND
OF
CHEROKEE INDIANS

1916

North Carolina Eastern Cherokee Census 1915-1922
June 30,1916 Taken by: James E. Henderson, Superintendent
1915-1916   Volume I

Number Last	Present	English Name	Relationship	Date of Birth	Sex
1	1	Ahnetonah, Nancy	Wid.	1837	F
2	2	Allen, Will	husb.	1845	M
3	3	" Sallie	wife	1851	F
4	4	Allen, John	husb.	1871	M
5	5	" Eve	wife	1884	F
6	6	" Welch Emeline	st-dau.	1901	F
7	7	Allison, Nannie I.	wife	1883	F
8	8	" Roy Robert	son	1904	M
9	9	" Albert Monroe	son	1907	M
10	10	" Ida May	dau.	1909	F
11	11	" Felix Wilbur	son	1912	M
12	12	Boyce Jackson	son	1914	M
13	13	Anderson, Addie I.G.	wife	1889	F
14	14	" Gertie	dau.	1910	F
15	15	Anderson, Louisa Jane	wife	1879	F
16	16	" Bessie	dau.	1902	F
17	17	" Cora	dau.	1904	F
18	18	" Ella	dau.	1910	F
19	19	" Wm. Burl	son	1912	M
20	20	Arch, Daivd[sic]	husb.	1859	M
21	21	" Martha	wife	1884	F
26	22	" Olivan	dau.	1894	F
22	23	" Ross	son	1896	M
23	24	" Jess	son	1908	M
24	25	" Jimmie	son	1910	M
25	26	(Arch), Eva Stella	dau.	1911	F
	27	" John Henderson	son	1916	M
27	28	" (Saunooke) Steve	ward	1897	M
28	29	Arch, Johnson son of No 20	husb.	1884	M
29	30	" Ella (nee Long)	wife	1890	F
30	31	" Cora	dau.	1908	F
31	32	" Horace	son	1909	M
32	33	" Elma	dau.	1911	F
33	34	" Bessie	Dau.	1915	F
34	35	Armachain, Amy separated	wife	1849	F
35	36	Armachain, Lacy	husb.	1876	M
36	37	" Anna	wife	1875	F
37	38	" James	son	1909	M
38	39	Armachain, Davis	husb.	1855	M
39	40	" Annie	wife	1871	F
41	41	" Louis	son	1898	M
42	42	" Rachel	dau.	1901	F

Number Last	Present	English Name	Relationship	Date of Birth	Sex
43	43	" Sevier	son	1904	M
40	44	Armachain, Jeese[sic] son of No. 39	husb.	1896	M
962	45	" Lucy (Long)	wife	1900	F
44	46	Armachain, Chewonih separated	husb.	1844	M
45	47	Arneach, Will West	widr	1849	M
47	48	" Buck West	son	1898	M
48	49	Arneach, Jefferson	husb.	1874	M
49	50	" Sarah	wife	1875	F
50	51	(Arneach) Margaret	dau.	1906	F
51	52	" Samuel	son	1909	M
52	53	" John E.H.	son	1911	M
53	54	" Sylvester S.	son	1914	M
54	55	" Stella P.	dau.	1913	F
55	56	" (Bird) Lizzie	st-dau.	1899	F
56	57	" " Bessie	st-dau.	1901	F
57	58	" " David	s-son	1894	M
58	59	Axe, Willie	widr	1871	M
59	60	" Maggie	dau.	1895	F
60	61	" Sarah	dau.	1896	F
61	62	Axe, John D.	husb.	1854	M
62	63	" Eve	wife	1864	F
63	64	Axe, Josiah	husb.	1864	M
64	65	" Sarah	wife	1881	F
65	66	" Nancy	dau.	1903	F
66	67	" Ella	dau.	1905	F
67	68	" Corinthia	dau.	1907	F
68	69	" Lazarus	son	1909	M
69	70	" Lulu	dau.	1910	F
70	71	" Dora	dau.	1913	F
71	72	" Cindy	dau.	1890	F
72	73	Baker, Almira	Wife	1872	f
73	74	" Dona	dau.	1895	f
74	75	" Crickett	son	1904	m
75	76	(Baker) Ben	son	1905	M
76	77	" Ada	dau.	1909	f
77	78	" Homer	son	1912	m
78	79	" Luther	son	1893	m
79	80	Baker, Ella C. Bruce	wife	1862	f
80	81	Baker, Ella McCoy	wife	1878	f
81	82	" Stella	dau.	1898	f
82	83	" Charlie W.	son	1902	m
83	84	" Mary R.	dau.	1905	f

Number		English Name	Relationship	Date of Birth	Sex
Last	Present				
84	85	" Cora	dau.	1910	f
85	86	" Alice	dau.	1913	f
86	87	Bates, Deliah, W. Smith	wife	1870	f
87	88	" Marshall Smith	son	1897	m
88	89	" Lizzie	dau.	1902	f
90	90	Batson, Henrietta Crowe	wife	1887	f
91	91	" Alfred G.	son	1911	m
92	92	" Olivan Jane	dau.	1914	f
93	93	Bearmeat, Mary	wid	1845	f
94	94	Ben, Cheick	husb.	1865	m
95	95	" Ollie	wife	1884	f
96	96	" Stan	son	1904	m
97	97	" Olivan	dau.	1906	f
98	98	" Candy	son	1911	m
99	99	" Callie	dau.	1913	f
1 [sic]	100	" Eyon	dau.	1915	f
100	101	Bigmeat, Robert	husb.	1894	m
101	102	" Charlotte L.C.	wife	?	f
102	103	" Minnie Crowe	dau.	1913	f
103	104	Bigmeat, Nicodemus	husb.	1875	m
104	105	" Nannie	wife	1865	f
105	106	Bigmeat, Yona	sing.	1877	m
106	107	" Ainihkih	widr.	1848	m
107	108	" Adam	son	1891	m
108	109	Bigmeat, Isaih[sic]	husb.	1878	m
109	110	Bigmeat, Sarah	wife	1882	f
110	111	" John	son	1912	m
111	112	Bird, Timson	sing.	1885	m
113	113	Bird, Ollie	wife	1882	f
114	114	" Annie	dau.	1906	f
115	115	" Lucy	Dau.	1909	f
116	116	" Minnie Woodpecker	dau.	1911	f
118	117	Bird, Lloyd	husb.	1883	m
119	118	Bird, Stephen	widr husb.	1853	m
121	119	Bird, Teheskie	husb.	1840	m
122	120	" Celia	wife	1853	f
123	121	Bird, Going	husb.	1869	m
124	122	" Annie	wife	1864	f
125	123	" Garfield (Tooni)	ward	1906	m
126	124	" Eli	son	1893	m
127	125	Blackfox, Cindy	wid	1842	f
128	126	Blackfox, Charlie	husb.	1879	m
129	127	" Nancy	wife	1883	f
130	128	" Lloyd	son	1903	m

North Carolina Eastern Cherokee Census 1915-1922
June 30,1916 Taken by: James E. Henderson, Superintendent
1915-1916   Volume I

Number Last	Present	English Name	Relationship	Date of Birth	Sex
131	129	" Nancy	dau.	1912	f
	130	" Ross	son	1912	m
133	131	Blackfox, Dinah G.	wid.	1857	f
134	132	" Keziah imbecile	s-son	1895	m
135	133	Blankenship, Arizona	wife	1875	f
136	134	" Lily J.	dau.	1909	f
137	135	" Fred	son	1911	m
138	136	" Leroy Edwin	son	1915	m
139	137	" Helen K.	dau.	1913	f
140	138	Blueowl,	widr.	1858	m
141	139	Blythe, Arch	husb.	1877	m
142	140	" Ida	wife	1881	f
143	141	" Sampson	son	1904	m
144	142	" Birdie Bell	dau.	1910	f
145	143	" Francis Marion	son	1913	m
x	144	" Baby	son	1916	m
146	145	Blythe, Wm. Henry	sing.	1876	m
147	146	Blythe, James	husb.	1861	m
148	147	" Fred (Bauer)	ward	1897	m
149	148	" Owena (Bauer)	ward	1895	f
150	149	Blythe, Jarrett	husb.	1886	m
151	150	" Mary B.	wife	1893	f
152	151	Blythe, David	husb.	1862	m
153	152	" Nancy	wife	1872	f
		chief[sic], was #149			
154	153	Blythe, Wm. Johnson	husb.	1872	m
155	154	" Lloyd	son	1909	m
	155	" Andy J.	son	1915	m
157	156	" Allen	son	1912	m
158	157	Bradley, Henry	husb.	1884	m
159	158	" Nancy	wife	1881	f
160	159	" James	son	1906	m
161	160	" Nancy	dau.	1908	f
162	161	" Arnessa	dau.	1909	f
163	162	" Shon	son	1911	m
164	163	" Goliath (George)	s-son	1902	m
165	164	Bradley, Eliza Jane	wife	1872	f
166	165	" Amos	son	1896	m
167	166	" Henry	son	1900	m
168	167	" Judson	son	1902	m
169	168	" Lydia	dau.	1905	f
170	169	" Seaborn	son	1907	m
171	170	" Bertha Anne	dau.	1910	f
172	171	" Wallace Russel	son	1912	m

North Carolina Eastern Cherokee Census 1915-1922
June 30,1916 Taken by: James E. Henderson, Superintendent
1915-1916 Volume I

Number Last	Present	English Name	Relationship	Date of Birth	Sex
173	172	Bradley, Nancy	sing.	1876	f
174	173	" Margaret	dau.	1899	f
175	174	" Roy	son	1903	m
176	175	" Minda	dau.	1905	f
177	176	(Bradley) Verdie W.	dau.	1909	f
178	177	Bradley, Annie	dau.	1902	f
179	178	" Dinah	dau.	1903	f
180	179	" Rachel	dau.	1906	f
181	180	" Thomas	son	1908	m
182	181	" Martha	dau.	1914	f
183	182	Bradley, Joseph	husb.	1881	m
184	183	" Bettie	dau.	1915	f
185	184	" Johnson	son	1909	m
186	185	" Lucinda	dau.	1912	f
187	186	" Louis	son	1913	m
188	187	" Walter	son	1902	m
189	188	" Nick	son	1895	m
190	189	" Morgan	son	1892	m
191	190	" Sarah	dau.	1900	f
192	191	Bradley, Johnson	husb.	1879	m
193	192	" Ethel	dau.	1910	f
195	193	Brady, Susie Smith	wife	1886	f
196	194	" James Lowen	son	1910	m
197	195	" Samuel	son	1912	m
198	196	" William	son	1913	m
199	197	Brady, Robert A.	Husb.	1868	m
200	198	" Eliza	dau.	1895	f
201	199	" Sarah	daug.	1897	f
202	200	" Arthur	son	1899	m
203	201	(Brady) McKinley	son	1902	m
204	202	" Luther	son	1904	m
205	203	" Elizabeth	dau.	1907	f
206	204	" Clyde	son	1908	m
207	205	" Callie	dau.	1911	f
208	206	Brewster, Linnie L.J.	wife	1892	f
209	207	" Elly	dau.	1910	f
210	208	Brown, Lydia	wid.	1847	f
211	209	Brown, Peter divorced	husb.	1883	m
212	210	" Nancy	wife	1883	f
213	211	Brown, Jonah	husb.	1881	m
214	212	" Agnes	wife	1881	f
215	213	" Mark	son	1910	m
216	214	" Lizzie	dau.	1912	f

North Carolina Eastern Cherokee Census 1915-1922
June 30,1916 Taken by: James E. Henderson, Superintendent
1915-1916   Volume I

Number Last	Present	English Name	Relationship	Date of Birth	Sex
	215	" Cain	son	1915	m
217	216	Bruce, Arthur	husb.	1890	m
218	217	Bruce, Thomas	husb.	1886	m
219	218	Bryant, Elizabeth H.G.	wife	1861	f
220	219	Burgess, Georgia Anne	wife	1869	f
221	220	" Bessie L.	dau.	1896	f
223	221	" Willie R.	dau.	1902	f
224	222	" George Alger	son	1906	m
225	223	" Nellie Luella	dau.	1909	f
226	224	" Frederick H.	son	1911	m
227	225	Bushyhead, Ben	husb.	1886	m
228	226	(Bushyhead) Nancy	wife	1887	f
229	227	" Joel	son	1911	m
230	228	" Robert	son	1914	m
231	229	Callaway, Bessie M. Nick	wife	1887	f
232	230	Calhoun, Morgan	husb.	1864	m
233	231	" Sallie Anne	wife	1877	f
234	232	" Eve	dau.	1898	f
235	233	" Yihginneh	dau.	1900	f
236	234	" Lawson	son	1902	m
237	235	" Holly	son	1904	m
238	236	" Sunday	son	1906	m
239	237	" Diana	dau.	1910	f
240	238	" Smathers	son	1912	m
	239	" Katie	dau.	1915	f
241	240	Calhoun, Polly	sing.	1894	f
242	241	Calhoun, Lawyer	husb.	1859	m
243	242	" Ollie	wife	1871	f
244	243	Cannaut, Abel	husb.	1880	m
245	244	" Susie	wife	1888	f
		divorced ?			
531	245	" Eliza Driver	wife	1871	f
246	246	Cannaut, Columbus	husb.	1884	m
247	247	" Maggie	wife	1890	f
		divorced			
248	248	" Minnie Goforth	wife	1887	f
249	249	" Louisa	s-dau.	1909	f
250	250	" Arthur	s-son	1911	m
251	251	(Cannaut) Addison	son	1909	m
252	252	Cat, Ben	husb.	1867	m
253	253	" Oney	wife	1860	f
254	254	Cat, Johnson	husb.	1859	m
255	255	" Sallie	wife	1861	f
864	256	" Margaret	dau.	1891	f

North Carolina Eastern Cherokee Census 1915-1922
June 30,1916 Taken by: James E. Henderson, Superintendent
1915-1916 Volume I

Number		English Name	Relationship	Date of Birth	Sex
Last	Present				
256	257	" Jesse	son	1895	m
257	258	" Amanda	dau.	1900	f
258	259	" Andy (Hornbuckle)	ward	1904	m
259	260	" Johnson	ward	1900	m
260	261	Cat, Willie	husb.	1887	m
261	262	" Corinthia	wife	1890	f
262	263	" David	son	1909	m
263	264	" Robert	son	1911	m
266	265	" Catolster, Wallace	husb.	1875	m
267	266	" Elsie F.	wife	1878	f
268	267	" Eliza	dau.	1913	f
269	268	" William	son	1879	m
270	269	Catolster, Carson	husb.	1891	m
271	269	" Josie	wife	1891	f
272	271	" Johnson	son	1909	m
273	272	" David	son	1910	m
274	273	" Margaret	dau.	1914	f
275	274	Catolster, Sallie	wife	1886	f
276	275	" Eliza Jane	dau.	1904	f
277	276	(Catolster) Alexander	son	1906	m
278	277	" Nannie	dau.	1909	f
279	278	" Gyon M	son	1910	m
280	279	" Lucy	dau.	1913	f
281	280	Cearley, Eucy Emmeline	wife	1879	f
282	281	" William Luther	son	1900	m
283	282	" Emery Lorenzo	son	1903	m
284	283	" Robert Astor	son	1905	m
285	284	" John Patrick	son	1911	m
	285	" Henry Thurman	son	1914	m
286	286	Chekelelee, Stone	husb.	1872	m
287	287	" Mary	wife	1863	f
288	288	" Simon	son	1899	m
289	289	" Rosa	dau.	1904	f
290	290	Chekelelee, Andy	husb.	1884	m
291	291	" Betty	wife	1889	f
292	292	" Bessie	dau.	1910	f
293	293	" Martha	dau	1912	f
294	294	Chekelelee, Tom	husb.	1866	m
295	295	" Luella	dau.	1905	f
296	296	" Wilson	son	1909	m
297	297	Childers. Lulu Frances	wife	1882	f
298	298	" Robert	son	1905	m
299	299	" Stella	dau.	1909	f
300	300	" Maud	dau.	1911	f

Number		English Name	Relationship	Date of Birth	Sex
Last	Present				
301	301	(Childers) Clifford E.	son	1913	m
302	302	Chiltoskie, Will	husb.	1858	m
303	303	" Charlotte	wife	1889	f
304	304	" Wahdih	son	1899	m
305	305	" James	son	1907	m
306	306	Clay, Timson imbecile	widr.	1873	m
307	307	" Arch (Teesateskie)	s-son	1897	m
308	308	" Awee	s-dau.	1900	f
309	309	" Jonah	s-son	1903	m
310	310	Clark, Lottie A.	wife	1869	f
313	311	Clingingbear,Ollie	wid.	1855	f
314	312	" Deliskie	son	1876	m
315	313	Cole, Geo. Wash.	husb.	1869	m
316	314	" Walter	son	1898	m
317	315	" Jewel	son	1900	m
318	316	" John	son	1904	m
319	317	" Lulu	dau.	1907	f
320	318	" Wilfred	son	1909	m
322	319	" Ida	dau.	1890	f
321	320	" Orna	dau.	1893	f
323	321	Cole, William A.	husb.	1879	m
324	322	" Arley	son	1905	m
325	323	" Hollie	son	1907	m
326	324	" Ollie	son	1909	m
327	325	" Attla	son	1910	m
328	326	Cole, Robert T.	husb.	1887	m
329	327	" Lloyd	son	1912	m
330	328	" George Emery	son	1891	m
331	329	Coleman, Harrison E.	husb.	1855	m
332	330	" Birdie A.	dau.	1896	f
333	331	" Lucius Calvin	son	1899	m
334	332	" Nancy M.E.	dau.	1890	f
335	333	Coleman, John N.	husb.	1872	m
336	334	" Julia N.	dau.	1904	f
337	335	" Henry J.	son	1906	m
338	336	Coleman, Geo. Wash.	husb.	1879	m
339	337	" Lillian M.	dau.	1906	f
340	338	" May Emmeline	dau.	1909	f
341	339	" Jesse James	son	1906	m
342	340	Coleman,William Edward	husb.	1881	m
343	341	" Julius Roosevelt	son	1904	m
344	342	" Sarah Eliza	dau.	1906	f
345	343	" Lily M.	dau.	1910	f
346	344	" William Robert	son	1912	m

North Carolina Eastern Cherokee Census 1915-1922
June 30,1916 Taken by: James E. Henderson, Superintendent
1915-1916   Volume I

Number Last	Present	English Name	Relationship	Date of Birth	Sex
347	345	Coleman, Simon Peter	husb.	1884	m
348	346	" Oscar	son	1910	m
349	347	" Otealve G.	dau.	1911	f
350	348	" Pearl May	dau.	1913	f
2211	349	" Valley	dau.	1915	f
351	350	Conley, John	widr.	1861	m
353	351	(Conley) John Jr.	son	1890	m
352	352	" Luke	son	1896	m
355	353	Conseen, Eliza G.	wid.	1893	f
356	354	" Annie G.	dau.	1913	f
1145	355	Conseen, Sally	wife	1871	f
1146	356	" Buck	son	1906	m
357	357	Conseen, Thompson	husb.	1891	m
358	358	" Irene A.	wife	1874	f
359	359	" Noah (Arch)	s-son	1895	m
360	360	" Codeskie "	s-son	1899	m
361	361	" Winnie (Arch)	s-dau.	1906	f
362	362	" Annie "	s-dau.	1909	f
363	363	Conseen, West	widr.	1862	m
364	364	" Dahney	dau.	1896	f
365	365	" Willie	son	1899	m
366	366	" James	son	1888	m
368	367	Conseen, Peter	husb.	1879	m
369	368	" Nancy	wife	1877	f
370	369	" Harry	son	1905	m
371	370	" Joe	son	1907	m
372	371	" Ida	dau.	1909	f
	372	" Nessie	dau.	1912	f
	373	" Solomon	son	1915	m
374	374	Conseen, Annie Arneach	wid.	1854	f
375	375	" Japson	son	1919	m
376	376	(Conseen) Kate	sing.	1864	f
377	377	" Martha	dau.	1898	f
378	378	Cook, Jessie Leora	wife	1891	f
379	379	" Vernie Lee	dau.	1909	f
380	380	" Inez Gertrude	dau.	1911	f
381	381	" Randall Edgar	son	1913	m
382	382	Cooper, Stacy Jane	wife	1868	f
391	383	" Arnold	son	1894	m
383	384	" Curtis	son	1896	m
384	385	" Frankie	dau.	1897	f
385	386	" Lelia	dau.	1898	f
386	387	" Fannie	dau.	1900	f
387	388	" Myrtle	dau.	1902	f

North Carolina Eastern Cherokee Census 1915-1922
June 30,1916 Taken by: James E. Henderson, Superintendent
1915-1916 Volume I

Number Last	Present	English Name	Relationship	Date of Birth	Sex
388	389	" Fred	son	1905	m
389	390	" Selma	dau.	1908	f
390	391	" Mary Joe	dau.	1910	f
396	392	Cornsilk, Famous	sing.	1912	m
		deceased - son of John C.			
397	393	Cornsilk, Armstrong	husb.	1852	m
398	394	" Annie	wife	1859	f
399	395	" Hettie	dau.	1898	f
400	396	" Howard	son	1900	m
401	397	Cornsilk, L. Dow	husb.	1881	m
402	398	" Nancy	wife	1882	f
403	399	" Woody	?	1909	m
404	400	" Emma	dau.	1911	f
405	401	(Cornsilk) Jacob	son	1914	m
406	402	Cornsilk, York	husb.	1867	m
407	403	" Eann	wife	1858	f
408	404	" Jennie (Saunooke)	ward	1903	f
413	405	Craig, William W.	husb.	1886	m
414	406	" Lillie V.	dau.	1914	f
415	407	Craig, Frank	husb.	1894	m
416	408	" Elvira H.	wife	1897	f
	409	" Robert Lee	son	1916	m
417	410	Crooks, Bessie Meroney	wife	1881	f
418	411	Crowe, Ute	husb.	1887	m
420	412	" Mary	wife	1873	f
421	413	" Callie	dau.	1904	f
422	414	" Albert	son	1906	m
423	415	" Lucy	dau.	1911	f
424	416	" Iva	dau.	1913	f
419	417	" Robert Henry	son	1914	m
425	418	Crowe, Caroline	wid.	1837	f
426	419	Crowe, Wesley R.	sing.	1875	m
427	420	Crowe, Joseph	husb.	1869	m
428	421	" Annie	wife	1865	f
429	422	" Boyd	son	1895	m
430	423	Crowe, John Wesley	husb.	1889	m
431	424	" Mollie Endros	wife	1878	f
432	425	" Joseph	son	1911	m
433	426	(Crowe) James David	son	1914	m
434	427	" Andros Edwin	s-son	1908	m
435	428	Crowe, David	husb.	1889	m
436	429	" Sallie	wife	1890	f
437	430	" Samuel	son	1907	m
438	431	" Rachel	dau.	1908	f

Number		English Name	Relationship	Date of Birth	Sex
Last	Present				
439	432	" Stacy	dau.	1909	f
440	433	" Nancy	dau.	1911	f
441	434	Crowe, Aquishoe	sing.	1888	m
442	435	Crowe, Arthur	husb.	1883	m
443	436	" Martha Toineeta	wife	1889	f
444	437	" Dinah	dau.	1913	f
	438	" Stacy	dau.	1916	f
445	439	Crowe, Sevier	husb.	1860	m
446	440	" Dora	dau.	1896	f
447	441	" Arthur	son	1899	m
448	442	" Luther	son	1899	m
449	443	" Lossi	son	1901	m
450	444	" Robert	son	1894	m
451	445	Cucumber, Dorcas	wid.	1851	f
452	446	" Dakie	dau.	1897	f
453	447	" William	son	1879	m
454	448	Cucumber, Gena	husb.	1881	m
455	449	" Katie	wife	1881	f
456	450	" Noah	sing.	1883	m
457	451	(Cucumber) Squinchey	son	1910	m
458	452	" Ollie (Saunooke)	s-dau.	1905	f
459	453	Cucumber, Arch	husb.	1888	m
460	454	" Ollie Youngbird	wife	1868	f
461	455	" James (Youngbird)	s-son	1900	m
462	456	" Walkinnih "	s-dau.	1905	f
463	457	Cucumber, James	husb.	1894	m
464	458	" Lizzie Reed	wife	1894	f
465	459	" Jennie	dau.	1911	f
466	460	" Macon	son	1913	m
467	461	Cucumber, Moses	widr.	1877	m
468	462	" John D.	son	1909	m
469	463	Dahnenolih or Smoke	widr.	1858	m
470	464	Dailey, Gita I.R.	wife	1891	f
	465	" Geneva	dau.	1915	f
472	466	Davis, Elsie	wid.	1853	f
473	467	Davis, Joe	husb.	1873	m
474	468	" Katie	wife	1858	f
475	469	Davis, Quaitih	wid.	1837	f
476	470	Davis, Rebecca	wife	1853	f
477	471	Davis, Charlie	husb.	1873	m
478	472	" Isaac	son	1899	m
479	473	" David	son	1901	m
480	474	" George	son	1905	m
481	475	" Callie	dau.	1909	f

North Carolina Eastern Cherokee Census 1915-1922
June 30,1916 Taken by: James E. Henderson, Superintendent
1915-1916   Volume I

Number Last	Present	English Name	Relationship	Date of Birth	Sex
482	476	(Davis) Israel	son	1894	m
483	477	Deaver, Mary E. Rob.	wife	1874	f
484	478	" John Robert	son	1909	m
485	479	Delegeskih, John	widr.	1851	m
486	480	" James (Taylor)	grson	1903	m
488	481	" Leander	grson	1906	m
489	482	" Taylor, John	grson	1909	m
491	483	Dobson, Mary George	wid.	1860	f
492	484	George, Kans	grson	1896	m
493	485	" Aggie Littlejohn	ward	1895	f
494	486	Dockery, Emma J. Payne	wife	1882	f
495	487	" Elsie Arlena	dau.	1906	f
496	488	" Ralph Burton	son	1908	m
497	489	" Cora	dau.	1910	f
498	490	" Dora Lee	dau.	1913	f
499	491	Donley, Robert L.	husb.	1872	m
500	492	" Sarah Eugenia	dau.	1914	f
501	493	Driver, Wesley	husb.	1872	m
502	494	" Agnes	wife	1870	f
503	495	" John	son	1899	m
504	496	" Lucinda	dau.	1902	f
505	497	" Sallie	dau.	1906	f
506	498	Driver, John Hill	husb.	1855	m
507	499	Driver, Sallie Calhoun	wife	1837	f
508	500	Driver, Judas	husb.	1869	m
509	501	(Driver) Eliza	wife	1868	f
510	502	" Annie divorced	wife	1845	f
511	503	Driver, Jimmie	husb.	1839	m
512	504	" Betty	wife	1843	f
513	505	Driver, Rusel E.	husb.	1874	m
514	506	" Marion	dau.	1904	f
515	507	" Elsie	dau.	1907	f
516	508	" Wesley	son	1912	m
517	509	Driver, Goliath B.	husb.	1876	m
518	510	" Helen Esther	dau.	1909	f
519	511	Driver, Chekelelee	husb.	1884	m
520	512	" Ollie	wife	1886	f
521	513	" Ross	dau.	1902	f
522	514	" George	son	1904	m
523	515	" Mason	son	1909	f
524	516	" Sag	son	1913	m
	517	" Amanda	dau.	1916	f
525	518	Driver, Dickey	husb.	1850	m

Number		English Name	Relationship	Date of Birth	Sex
Last	Present				
526	519	" Etta	wife	1879	f
527	520	" Nannie	dau.	1906	f
528	521	" Dehart	son	1909	m
529	522	" John	son	1912	m
530	523	" William	son	1873	m
532	524	Driver, Ned son of No. 245	son	1897	m
533	525	" Driver, Adam	son	1901	m
534	526	Duncan, Lillian V.	wife	1877	f
535	527	" Sybil	dau.	1906	f
536	528	Eubank, Lillie	wife	1888	f
537	529	" Joseph	son	1906	m
538	530	" Lillie M.	dau.	1908	f
539	531	" Verlin R.	son	1909	m
540	532	" Clarence	son	1911	m
541	533	Feather, Lawyer	husb.	1863	m
542	534	" Mary	wife	1869	f
543	535	" Gahtayah	dau.	1900	f
544	536	" Jonah	son	1906	m
545	537	Featherhead, Wilson	husb.	1876	m
546	538	" Nancy	wife	1844	f
547	539	Finger, Sophronia C.	wife	1876	f
548	540	" Samuel A.	son	1898	m
549	541	" Leonia	dau.	1905	f
550	542	" Elmer Eugene	son	1908	m
551	543	" Ruby Irene	dau.	1911	f
553	544	Foxsquirrel imbecile	sing.	1859	m
554	545	Fodder, Jennie	wid.	1842	f
555	546	" Daniel Hornbuckle	grson	1896	m
556	547	Fortner, Sis	wife	1871	f
557	548	Foster, Alice	wife	1876	f
558	549	" Elsie	dau.	1899	f
559	550	" Robert	son	1901	m
560	551	(Foster) Burton	son	1903	m
561	552	" Leroy	son	1906	m
562	553	French, Linda Otter	wid.	1894	f
563	554	French, Awee	wife	1878	f
564	555	" Meroney	son	1897	m
565	556	" Morgan	son	1900	m
566	557	" Soggie	son	1902	m
567	558	" George	son	1905	m
568	559	" Jonah	son	1907	m
569	560	" Lizzie	dau.	1909	f
570	561	French, Wallie divorced	wife	1880	f

North Carolina Eastern Cherokee Census 1915-1922
June 30,1916 Taken by: James E. Henderson, Superintendent
1915-1916   Volume I

Number Last	Present	English Name	Relationship	Date of Birth	Sex
571	562	" Ned	son	1900	m
572	563	" Nellie	dau.	1902	f
573	564	" Katie	dau.	1907	f
574	565	" Jesse	son	1905	m
575	566	Garland, Elizabeth	wid.	1830	f
576	567	Garland, Tullius B.	husb.	1850	m
577	568	Garland, John Basco	husb.	1879	m
578	569	" Frank	son	1906	m
579	570	" Fred	son	1908	m
580	571	" Edgar	son	1911	m
581	572	Garland, Roxiana	dau.	1858	f
582	573	Garland, Elizabeth	dau.	1887	f
583	574	Garland, William S.	son	1866	m
584	575	Garland, Jesse L.	husb.	1856	m
585	576	(Garland) Emery	son	1903	m
586	577	" Rady Elmer	dau.	1906	f
587	578	Garland, Leonze	husb.	1885	m
588	579	" Honelee	son	1910	m
590	580	George, Dawson	husb.	1860	m
591	581	" Mary	wife	1859	f
592	582	" Annie	dau.	1883	f
593	583	" Manly	son	1890	m
594	584	George, Davis	husb.	1851	m
595	585	" Rosa E. Biddicks	wife	1879	f
596	586	" Jennie (Biddicks)	s-dau.	1903	f
597	587	" Polly "	s-dau.	1907	f
598	588	George, Shon	sing.	1871	m
599	589	George, Elijah	husb.	1874	m
600	590	" Nancy Wilnoty	wife	1887	f
601	591	" Aggie	s-dau.	1906	f
602	592	" Nancy	s-dau.	1907	f
603	593	" Louis	son	1904	m
604	594	" Martha	dau.	1905	f
605	595	" Cornelia	dau.	1907	f
606	596	" Letta	dau.	1911	f
607	597	Goerge,[sic] Green	sing.	1899	m
609	598	George, Elizabeth	wife	1859	f
610	599	George, Jacob	husb.	1897	m
612	600	George, Celia	dau.	1900	f
613	601	George, Jackson	son	1903	m
614	602	George, Bessie Taylor	wid.	1897	f
615	603	" Amanda	dau.	1911	f
616	604	George, Esller[sic]	wid.	1856	f
617	605	George, Elijah	sing.	1877	m

North Carolina Eastern Cherokee Census 1915-1922
June 30,1916 Taken by: James E. Henderson, Superintendent
1915-1916   Volume I

Number Last	Present	English Name	Relationship	Date of Birth	Sex
618	606	George, Logan	son	1888	m
619	607	George, Julia V.	wife	1875	m[sic]
620	608	" Lottie B.	dau.	1906	f
621	609	" Wallace L.	son	1908	m
622	610	George, Shell	sing.	1860	m
623	611	Goin, Sallie	dau.	1849	f
624	612	Goin, Birdchopper	husb.	1869	m
625	613	" Ollie	wife	1872	f
626	614	" Daniel	son	1899	m
627	615	" Emmeline	dau.	1909	f
629	616	Going, Snake	husb.	1857	m
630	617	" Nancy	wife	1866	f
631	618	Graybeard, Lillie	sing.	1892	f
632	619	Graybeard, Ezekial	sing.	1840	m
633	620	Graybeard, Aggie	sing.	1850	f
634	621	Green, Cora E.? Payne	wife	1884	f
635	622	" Lurlie Beatrice	dau.	1907	f
636	623	" Bonnie Lee	dau.	1912	f
	624	" Willie	son	1914	m
637	625	" Blanche J.	dau.	1912	f
638	626	Griffin, Daisy Yonce	wife	1892	f
639	627	" Nola	dau.	1911	f
640	628	" Ima	dau.	1913	f
409	629	Harding., Mary J.? Craig	wife	1877	f
410	630	Robert Donley C.	son	1905	m
411	631	" Harold	son	1912	m
412	632	" Florence S.	dau.	1914	f
	633	" Louis Emmet	son	1915	m
641	634	Hawkins, Dora Parilee	wife	1882	f
642	635	" Charlie Leonard	son	1904	m
643	636	" Luther	son	1909	m
644	637	" Delia May	dau.	1911	f
645	638	Hill, Soggy M.	husb.	1881	m
646	639	" Henrietta	wife	1874	f
647	640	Hill, Maul divorced	husb.	1847	m
648	641	Hill, Blaine	husb.	1886	m
649	642	" Luzene	wife	1883	f
651	643	" Viola Nellie	dau.	1909	f
652	644	" Birdie Charlotte	dau.	1911	f
	645	" Blaine Jr.	son	1915	m
650	646	Ammons Sequoyah	s-son	1905	m
653	647	Hill, Ned	sing.	1888	m
654	648	Hill, Levi	husb.	1890	m

North Carolina Eastern Cherokee Census 1915-1922
June 30,1916 Taken by: James E. Henderson, Superintendent
1915-1916   Volume I

Number		English Name	Relationship	Date of Birth	Sex
Last	Present				
655	649	" Laura Jane Wolfe	wife	1890	f
656	650	" Lawrence	son	1913	m
657	651	Hill, Abraham	husb.	1864	m
658	652	" Annie	wife	1872	f
659	653	" Hensley	son	1899	m
660	654	" Callie	dau.	1902	f
661	655	Holland, Jennie	wife	1886	f
662	656	" Grace	dau.	1904	f
663	657	" David	son	1909	m
664	658	Hornbuckle, Rebecca	wid.	1848	f
665	659	Hornbuckle, Maggie	sing.	1880	f
666	660	Hornbuckle, Israel	son	1885	m
667	661	Hornbuckle, William	husb.	1882	m
668	662	" Jennie	wife	1886	f
669	663	" Clarence	son	1910	m
670	664	" Nora	dau.	1912	f
671	665	Hornbuckle, John Otto	husb.	1871	m
672	666	" Mattie	wife	1865	f
673	667	" Dahnih	dau.	1905	f
674	668	Hornbuckle, Caroline	wid.	1860	f
675	669	Hornbuckle, John L.	husb.	1884	m
676	670	" Martha	wife	1882	f
677	671	" Ben	son	1913	m
678	672	Hornbuckle, Jeff Davis	widr.	1864	m
679	673	" Jeff Davis Jr.	son	1892	m
680	674	Hornbuckle, George	husb.	1877	m
681	675	" Melissa	dau.	1896	f
682	676	(Hornbuckle) Alice May	dau.	1898	f
683	677	" Hartman	son	1901	m
684	678	" Olive Anne	dau.	1903	f
685	679	" John Russel	son	1905	m
686	680	" Wm. Allen	son	1908	m
687	681	" Clifford	son	1910	m
688	682	" Thurman	son	1912	m
	683	" Clyda May	dau.	1915	f
689	684	Hornbuckle, William	husb.	1870	m
690	685	" Fred	son	1896	m
691	686	" Dora	dau.	1899	f
		div. wife of Robert Crowe			
692	687	" Wilson	son	1901	m
693	688	" Maggie	dau.	1905	f
694	689	" Jennie	dau.	1911	f
696	690	Jackson, John	husb.	1836	m
697	691	" Stacy	wife	1846	f

North Carolina Eastern Cherokee Census 1915-1922
June 30,1916 Taken by: James E. Henderson, Superintendent
1915-1916   Volume I

Number		English Name	Relationship	Date of Birth	Sex
Last	Present				
698	692	" Jack	son	1892	m
699	693	Jackson, Lawyer	husb.	1873	m
700	694	" Dakie	wife	1871	f
701	695	" Florence	dau.	1903	f
702	696	" Ella	dau.	1895	f
703	697	Jackson, Eliza	wid.	1848	f
704	698	Jackson, Bob	husb.	1876	m
705	699	" Caroline	wife	1880	f
706	700	" Wesley	son	1900	m
707	701	(Jackson) David	son	1902	m
708	702	" Eddie	son	1904	m
709	703	" Ikee	son	1909	m
	704	" Samuel	son	1914	m
710	705	Jackson, Jacob	husb.	1894	m
	706	" Amanda	wife	?	f
		maiden name?			
	707	" Hattie	dau.	1915	f
711	708	Jessan, Lydia	wid.	1855	f
712	709	" Joseph	son	1894	m
713	710	Jessan, Dahnola	husb.	1880	f
46	711	" Nellie West	wife	1896	f
714	712	" Elnora	dau.	1909	f
715	713	" Lillian	dau.	1910	f
716	714	" John J. Astor	son	1913	m
717	715	Johnson, Jim	sing.	1850	m
718	716	Johnson, Addison	sing.	1886	m
719	717	Johnson, Yona	husb.	1880	m
720	718	" Dora	wife	1884	f
721	719	" Frank T.R.	son	1909	m
722	720	" Margaret G.	dau.	1912	f
723	721	Johnson, Jimpsie	husb.	1874	m
724	722	" Ella	wife	1858	f
725	723	Johnson, Stephen	husb.	1846	m
726	724	" Jennie	wife	1850	f
727	725	" Sim Dehart Jessan	grson	1904	m
728	726	Johnson, Taskigee	husb.	1878	m
729	727	" Sallie Oosowee	wife	1878	f
731	728	" Oosowee, Tahquette	st-son	1899	m
732	729	Johnson, Jane (Jennie)	wid.	1889	f
733	730	" Tom	son	1909	m
734	731	" Jonah	son	1911	m
735	732	Johnson, Tempa	dau.	1890	f
736	733	Johnson, Isaac	son	1893	m
737	734	Jumper, Ute	husb.	1873	m

Number		English Name	Relationship	Date of Birth	Sex
Last	Present				
738	735	" Betsey	wife	1874	f
739	736	" Stansil	son	1899	m
740	737	" Edward	son	1901	m
741	738	" James U.	son	1904	m
742	739	" Thomas	son	1906	m
743	740	" Henry	son	1908	m
744	741	" Ella	dau.	1909	f
745	742	" Sarah	dau.	1913	f
746	743	Junaluskie, Jim	son	1892	m
747	744	Jordon, William Clark	husb.	1848	m
748	745	" Alfred	son	1894	m
749	746	" Ollie (Hodges)	wife	1895	f
750	747	" William	son	1888	m
751	748	Kalonuheskie, Esiah	widr.	1855	m
752	749	" Martha	dau.	1902	f
753	750	Kalonaheskie, Tom	husb.	1888	m
1651	751	(Kolonaheskie)[sic], Eve S. nee Smoker	wife	1897	f
754	752	Kolonaheskie, Abraham	husb.	1884	m
755	753	Kolonaheskie, Charlie	husb.	1886	m
960	754	" Sallie children Nos. 965-970 nee Long	wife	1877	f
756	755	Kolonaheskie, Joe	son	1888	m
758	756	Keg, Katie	wid.	1857	f
759	757	Keg, Matthew	husb.	1866	m
760	758	" Rebecca	dau.	1910	f
761	759	" Fannie	dau.	1914	f
762	760	Key, Delia Anne	wife	1891	f
763	761	" William H.	son	1910	m
764	762	" Clarence E.	son	1912	m
	763	" Nola May	dau.	1915	f
765	764	Kunteeskih	husb.	1850	m
766	765	" Sahwahchi	wife	1846	f
767	766	" Bird (Waidsutte)	neph	1910	m
768	767	Ladd, Bonney Rogers	wife	1892	f
769	768	" Mark	son	1911	m
770	769	Lambert, John M.	husb.	1862	m
771	770	Lambert., Lloyd	husb.	1883	m
772	771	" Sallie	wife	1880	f
773	772	" Luzene	s-dau.	1901	f
774	773	" Ollie	dau.	1905	f
775	774	" Nellie	dau.	1907	f
776	775	" Richard	son	1909	m
777	776	(Lambert) Ruth	dau.	1913	f

Number		English Name	Relationship	Date of Birth	Sex
Last	Present				
778	777	Lambert, Charlie	husb.	1886	m
779	778	" Mary Arch	wife	1887	f
780	779	" Jackson	son	1906	m
781	780	" John Adam	son	1911	m
782	781	" Luvenia	dau.	1913	f
783	782	Lambert, Hugh Nolan	husb.	1882	m
784	783	" Alice Rosa	wife	1884	f
785	784	" Paul Leroy	son	1909	m
786	785	" Arthur J.	son	1911	m
787	786	" Albert Smith	son	1914	m
	787	" Mary Emma	dau.	1916	f
788	788	Lambert, Thomas R.	husb.	1874	m
789	789	" Nannie	wife	1888	f
790	790	" Florence	dau.	1908	f
791	791	" Seymour	son	1909	m
792	792	Lambert, Samuel C.	husb.	1860	m
793	793	" Verdie	dau.	1895	m
794	794	" Corbett	son	1897	m
795	795	" Cora Lee	dau.	1900	f
796	796	" Julia	dau.	1901	f
797	797	" Theodore	son	1904	m
798	798	" Oney	dau.	1906	f
799	799	" Gaylord	son	1909	m
800	800	" Lillian N.	dau.	1912	f
	801	(Lambert) Russel	son	1916	m
801	802	Lambert, Nannie (Hipps)	wife	1893	f
802	803	" Nina Marie	dau.	1913	f
803	804	Lambert, Claudie	husb.	1891	m
804	805	Lambert, Albert J.	husb.	1852	m
805	806	Lambert, Jesse B.	husb.	1877	m
806	807	" Minnie Stiles	wife	1890	f
807	808	" Carl Glenn	son	1911	m
808	809	" Jessie Evelyn	dau.	1914	f
809	810	Lambert, James W.	husb.	1875	m
810	811	" Bessie	dau.	1900	f
811	812	" Hugh H.	son	1902	m
812	813	" Ida M.	dau.	1909	f
813	814	" Lulu	dau.	1911	f
814	815	" Mintha A.	dau.	1913	f
8[sic]	816	" Buna	dau.	1915	f
815	817	Lambert, Thomas O.	husb.	1879	m
816	818	" Joseph C.	son	1903	m
817	819	" Henry H.	son	1904	m
818	820	" John A.	son	1906	m

North Carolina Eastern Cherokee Census 1915-1922
June 30,1916 Taken by: James E. Henderson, Superintendent
1915-1916   Volume I

Number Last	Present	English Name	Relationship	Date of Birth	Sex
819	821	Sallie M.	dau.	1909	f
820	822	" Nellie	dau.	1911	f
	823	" Cora Hazel	dau.	1913	f
	824	" Gracie N.	dau.	1915	f
821	825	Lambert, Columbus	husb.	1870	m
822	826	(Lambert) Harvey	son	1897	m
823	827	" Carson	son	1904	m
824	828	Lambert, Hugh J.	husb.	1874	m
825	829	" Pearl B.	dau.	1899	f
826	830	" Andrew J.	son	1901	m
827	831	" Isaac	son	1903	m
828	832	" Dora	dau.	1908	f
829	833	" George	son	1909	m
830	834	" Pearson	ward	1899	m
831	835	" Ethel	dau.	1912	f
832	836	Lambert, J. Monroe	husb.	1857	m
833	837	" Jesse	son	1895	m
834	838	" Fitzsimmons	son	1897	m
835	839	" Flora	grdau.	1901	f
836	840	" Maney Minnie Araminta	grdau.	1905	f
837	841	" " Ruth	grdau.	1907	f
838	842	" " Bruce Garret	grson	1909	m
839	843	Lambert, Fred	husb.	1893	m
840	844	Lambert, Charles	son	1893	m
841	845	Lambert, Joseph Jackson	husb.	1895	m
842	846	" Cora Palestine	dau.	1906	f
843	847	" Leonard Carson	son	1908	m
844	848	" Willard	son	1910	m
845	849	" Gillian	son	1912	m
846	850	" Lena	dau.	1915	f
847	851	(Lambert)Edward Monroe	son	1907	m
848	852	Lambert, Ed	husb.	1847	m
849	853	Larch, William	sing.	1876	m
850	854	Larch, David	sing.	1883	m
852	855	Lee, William Clyde dead, son of Samuel L.	sing.	1912	m
	856	Lee, James Floyd	sing.	1914	m
853	857	Lee, Debreda	sing.	1899	f
854	858	Lee, Edith	sing.	1896	f
855	859	Lee, Alonzo	husb.	1874	m
856	860	" Alice May	dau.	1902	f
857	861	" Myrtle Gert	dau.	1907	f
858	862	Ledford, Sampson	husb.	1885	m
	863	" Nicey	dau.	1916	f

North Carolina Eastern Cherokee Census 1915-1922
June 30,1916 Taken by: James E. Henderson, Superintendent
1915-1916   Volume I

Number		English Name	Relationship	Date of Birth	Sex
Last	Present				
859	864	Ledford, Charlie	husb.	1883	m
860	865	" Maggie Walk	wife	1892	f
861	866	Ledford, Jake	husb.	1874	m
862	867	" Mary	wife	1885	f
863	868	" Amy	dau.	1908	f
864	869	Ledford, Onih	wid.	1853	f
865	870	Ledford, Riley	husb.	1875	m
866	871	" Polly	wife	1882	f
867	872	" Joe	son	1901	m
868	873	" Kina	dau.	1903	f
869	874	" Caroline	dau.	1907	f
870	875	" Willie	son	1909	m
871	876	Ledford, Caroline M.R.	wife	1884	f
872	877	" Minnie	dau.	1896	f
873	878	" Cora	dau.	1903	f
874	879	" Adkins	son	1906	m
875	880	" Charles Alvin	son	1908	m
876	881	" Bonnie Marie	dau.	1910	f
877	882	" Cyrus Atlas	son	1912	m
878	883	" Iowa	dau.	1894	f
552	884	Leo, Ramona C. Finger	wife	1896	f
879	885	Le Fevers, Temoxzenah G.	wife	1881	f
880	886	" Linnie	dau.	1900	f
881	887	" William	son	1901	m
882	888	Littlejohn, Saunooke	husb.	1863	m
883	889	" Anne Eliza	wife	1868	f
884	890	" Henson	son	1899	m
885	891	" John	son	1902	m
886	892	" Owen	son	1906	m
887	893	" Addie	dau.	1908	f
888	894	" Emmeline	dau.	1909	f
889	895	Littlejohn, Wiggins	husb.	1891	m
890	896	" Caroline S.	wife	1888	f
891	897	" Sallie A. (Stdgdr) deceased?	s-dau.	1909	f
892	898	" Edgar J.	son	1913	m
894	899	Littlejohn, Guy son of Will L.	sing.	1897	m
895	900	Littlejohn, Katie dau. of Will L.	sing.	1898	f
896	901	Littlejohn, Isaac	sing.	1900	m
897	902	Littlejohn, Elowih	husb.	1875	m
898	903	" Annie	wife	1879	f
899	904	" Sallie Anne	dau.	1902	f

North Carolina Eastern Cherokee Census 1915-1922
June 30,1916 Taken by: James E. Henderson, Superintendent
1915-1916   Volume I

Number		English Name	Relationship	Date of Birth	Sex
Last	Present				
900	905	" Sherman	son	1904	m
901	906	" Jefferson	son	1907	m
902	907	" Wesley	son	1909	m
903	908	" Lizzie	dau.	1913	f
904	909	" Rachel Tooni	ward	1899	f
905	910	" Minda	dau.	1912	f
906	911	" George Goolarche	ward	1902	m
907	912	Littlejohn, Ropetwister	husb.	1865	m
908	913	" Annie	wife	1877	f
909	914	" Joseph (Wilnoty)	s-son	1895	m
910	915	" Ned "	s-son	1896	m
911	916	" Sallie	Dau.	1901	f
912	917	" Isaac	son	1906	m
913	918	" Eugene	son	1912	m
914	919	" Bessie	dau.	1914	f
915	920	Littlejohn, Goliath	husb.	1870	m
916	921	Locust, John	husb.	1852	m
917	922	" Polly Anne	wife	1856	f
918	923	Locust, Noah	husb.	1882	m
919	924	" Louis	son	1901	m
920	925	" Laura B.	dau.	1903	f
921	926	(Locust) Tiny	dau.	1905	f
922	927	" Martha	dau.	1910	f
923	928	" Homer	son	1911	m
924	929	" Josephine	dau.	1913	f
	930	" Wm. Arthur	son	1915	m
925	931	Long, Adam	husb.	1847	m
926	932	" Polly	wife	1856	f
927	933	" Eve	dau.	1898	f
928	934	" Nola	dau.	1901	f
929	936	Long, Joe	husb.	1858	m
930	936	" Nancy George	wife	1839	f
931	937	" Charlie	son	1894	m
932	938	Long, Peter	husb.	1879	m
933	939	" Anona C.	wife	1890	f
934	940	Long, Rachel (Harris)	wife	1883	f
935	941	Long, Dobson	husb.	1858	m
936	942	" Sallie	wife	1870	f
937	943	" Wm. Gaffney	son	1897	m
938	944	" Elizabeth	dau.	1901	f
939	945	Long, Johnson	husb.	1862	m
940	946	" Maggie	wife	1876	f
941	947	" Annie	dau.	1907	f
942	948	Long, Scott	husb.	1852	m

Number Last	Present	English Name	Relationship	Date of Birth	Sex
943	949	" Sallie	wife	1862	f
944	950	" Anita (Davis)	s-dau.	1897	f
946	951	(Long) Agginy	dau.	1905	f
947	952	Long, John	husb.	1873	m
948	953	" Eve	wife	1865	f
949	954	Long, Rachel	sing.	1874	f
950	955	Long, Joseph Bigwitch	husb.	1882	m
951	956	" Sallie	wife	1879	f
952	957	" Alice (Crowe)	s-dau.	1897	f
953	958	" Lucy	dau.	1905	f
954	959	" Etta	dau.	1907	f
955	960	" Lloyd	son	1909	m
956	961	" John	son	1911	m
957	962	Long, Nellie	wid.	1844	f
958	963	" Charlie Bigwitch	son	1888	m
959	964	Long, Jackson	husb.	1855	m
961	965	Long, Longbear	son	1898	m
963	966	Long, Aggie child of 754	dau.	1902	f
964	967	Long, Betty child of 754	dau.	1904	f
965	968	Long, Isaac child of 754	son	1906	m
966	969	Long, Lena child of 754	dau.	1908	f
967	970	Long, Martha child of 754	dau.	1913	f
968	971	Long, Will West	husb.	1871	m
969	972	" Annie Welch	wife	1891	f
970	973	Lossih, John Dehart	husb.	1870	m
971	974	" Laura	wife	1870	f
972	975	" John Jr.	son	1898	m
973	976	(Lossih) Jesse James	son	1907	m
974	977	" Jonas	son?	1909	m
975	978	" Lizzie	dau.	1891	f
976	979	Lossih, Henry	husb.	1871	m
977	980	" Aggie	wife	1880	f
978	981	Lossih, Rosa	dau.	1907	f
979	982	" Cawell	son	1909	m
980	983	" Abel	son	1911	m
981	984	" Mary	dau.	1913	f
	985	" Josiah	son	1915	m
982	986	" McKinley (Ross)	s-son	1901	m

Number Last	Present	English Name	Relationship	Date of Birth	Sex
983	987	Lossih, Jonas	husb.	1873	m
984	988	" Nicey	wife	1880	f
985	989	" Tom (Walkingstick)	ward	1908	m
986	990	" Lossih, Jennie	wid.	1858	f
987	991	" Dom Thomas	son	1896	m
988	992	" Candy	son	1898	m
989	993	" John R.	son	1903	m
990	994	" Hayes	son	1905	m
991	995	" David	son	189	m
992	996	" Leander	son	1885	m
993	997	Loudermilk, Josephine G.	wife	1877	f
994	998	" Nora	dau.	1902	f
995	999	" Elmer	son	1902	m
996	1000	" Cora	dau.	1906	f
997	1001	(Loudermilk) Clinton	son	1908	m
998	1002	Loudermilk, Cynthia A.	wife	1861	f
999	1003	" Rebecca	dau.	1899	f
1000	1004	Loudermilk, John R.	husb.	1879	m
1001	1005	" Luther	son	1900	m
1002	1006	" William R.	son	1904	m
1003	1007	" Julia	dau.	1906	f
1004	1008	" Leroy	son	1909	m
1005	1009	" Wilford Thurston	son	1913	m
1006	1010	Lowen, John B.	sing.	1861	m
1007	1011	Lowen, John	husb.	1861	m
1008	1012	" Sis	wife	1862	m
1009	1013	" Nannie (Kolonaheskie)s-dau.		1897	f
1010	1014	Maney, Eva	wife	1896	f
1011	1015	" Mary	dau.	1904	f
1012	1016	" John	son	1906	m
1013	1017	" Allen Jacob	son	1918	m
1014	1018	" Alice	dau.	1910	f
1015	1019	" Caroline	dau.	1913	f
	1020	" Simon Joshua	son	1914	m
1016	1021	Martin, Suate	widr.	1856	m
1017	1022	Martin, Thomas	husb.	1887	m
945	1023	" Emmeline Davis	wife	1900	f
1018	1024	Martin, George	husb.	1861	m
1019	1025	" Lucy	wife	1872	f
1020	1026	(Martin) Charles	son	1908	m
1021	1027	Martin, Wesley	husb.	1895	m
1023	1028	Mashburn, Harriet A.	wife	1878	f
1024	1029	" Mindy (Littlejohn)	dau.	1894	f
1025	1030	" Manco (Murphy)	son	1891	m

North Carolina Eastern Cherokee Census 1915-1922
June 30,1916 Taken by: James E. Henderson, Superintendent
1915-1916   Volume I

Number		English Name	Relationship	Date of Birth	Sex
Last	Present				
1026	1031	" Frank	son	1900	m
1027	1032	" Bessie	dau.	1901	f
1028	1033	" James L.	son	1904	m
1029	1034	" Sarah	dau.	1906	f
1030	1035	" Thomas	son	1911	m
	1036	" Loraine	dau.	1915	f
1031	1037	Mashburn, Leora	wife	1884	f
1032	1038	" Minnie	dau.	1902	f
1033	1039	" Mattie	dau.	1904	f
1034	1040	" Bertha	dau.	1907	f
1035	1041	" Ninia	dau.	1908	f
1036	1042	Matthews, Lillian W.L.	wife	1881	f
1037	1043	" Eva Addie	dau.	1905	f
1038	1044	" Grady R.	son	1908	m
1039	1045	" Mary Laurena	dau.	1911	f
1040	1046	McAllister, Harriet A.G.	wife	1866	f
1041	1047	McCoy, David	husb.	1873	m
1042	1048	" Marinda	dau.	1900	f
1043	1049	" James	s-one[sic]	1902	m
1044	1050	" Julia	dau.	1904	f
1045	1051	(McCoy) Stella	dau.	1906	f
1046	1052	" Jesse	son	1910	m
1047	1053	" Bessie	dau.	1911	f
1048	1054	" Eva	dau.	1913	f
1049	1055	McCoy, John	husb.	1875	m
1050	1056	" Pearson	son	1897	m
1051	1057	" Mary	dau.	1901	f
1052	1058	" James	son	1905	m
1053	1059	" Walter	son	1909	m
1054	1060	McCoy, James	husb.	1881	m
1055	1061	" William C.	son	1905	m
1056	1062	" Joseph H.	son	1907	m
1057	1063	" Frank	son	1912	m
1058	1064	McLeymore, John L.	husb.	1854	m
1059	1065	" Cora May	dau.	1905	f
1060	1066	McLeymore, Samuel H.	husb.	1855	m
1061	1067	" Morrell	son	1901	m
1062	1068	" Samuel Ross	son	1906	m
1063	1069	" Elsie Bonnie	dau.	1909	f
1064	1070	" William Glen	son	1910	m
1065	1071	" Kimmit E.	son	1913	m
1067	1072	Meroney, John G.	husb.	1865	m
1068	1073	" Sallie Belle	dau.	1895	f
1069	1074	" Mays	dau.	1897	f

North Carolina Eastern Cherokee Census 1915-1922
June 30,1916 Taken by: James E. Henderson, Superintendent
1915-1916   Volume I

Number Last	Present	English Name	Relationship	Date of Birth	Sex
1070	1075	" Gertrude	dau.	1899	f
1071	1076	(Meroney) Bailey B.	son	1901	m
1072	1077	" Della	dau.	1906	f
1078	1078	Meronry, Bailey Barton	husb.	1866	m
1079	1079	" Margaret A.	dau.	1899	f
1080	1080	" Richard B.	son	1902	m
1081	1081	" Felix	son	1904	m
1082	1082	" William H.	son	1907	m
1083	1083	" Raymond	son	1913	m
1084	1084	Miller, Flourney Rogers	wife	1889	f
1085	1085	" Vessey	dau.	1908	f
1086	1086	" Bessie	dau.	1909	f
1087	1087	" Vertie	dau.	1911	f
1216	1088	Moody, Callie Owl	wife	1888	f
1217	1089	" Harlan	dau.	1914	f
	1090	" Garland Edward	son	1915	m
1088	1091	Monroe, Nora A.	wife	1880	f
1089	1092	" Charles A.	son	1907	m
1090	1093	" Hugh N.	son	1910	m
1091	1094	Mumblehead, John D.	husb.	1864	m
1092	1095	" Dahney	wife	1881	f
1093	1096	" Roger L.	son	1896	m
1094	1097	" Elizabeth	dau.	1906	f
1095	1098	" James B.	son	1889	m
1096	1099	" James W.	son	1880	m
1098	1100	Murphy, Fred	sing.	1907	m
1099	1101	Murphy, Howard	sing.	1894	m
1100	1102	Murphy, Louisa	sing.	1886	f
1101	1103	Murphy, Margaret	sing.	1888	f
1102	1104	Murphy, Isabella	sing.	1890	f
1103	1105	Murphy, Jesse	husb.	1863	m
1104	1106	" Mary McC.	wife	1877	f
1105	1107	" Lillian Arch cousin of 1106	sing.	1905	f
1106	1108	Murphy, William	husb.	1890	m
1107	1109	" Lafayette	son	1910	m
1108	1110	" Robert	son	1912	m
1109	1111	Murphy, David	husb.	1830	m
1110	1112	Murphy, Joseph Marion	husb.	1864	m
1111	1113	" Cynthia Minerva	dau.	1895	f
1112	1114	" Clifford	grson	1904	m
1113	1115	Garret, Lily A. Murphy	wife	1880	f
1114	1116	" Alger	son	1908	m
1115	1117	" Hollie	dau.	1909	f

Number		English Name	Relationship	Date of Birth	Sex
Last	Present				
1116	1118	" Allen	son	1912	m
1117	1119	" Mary J.	dau.	1881	f
1118	1120	Patterson, Eustice J.M.	wife	1885	f
1119	1121	" Bob	son	1905	m
1120	1122	" May	dau.	1906	f
1121	1123	Stroud, Flora B.M. Murphy	wife	1887	f
1122	1124	" Dessie	dau.	1909	f
1123	1125	" Ethel	dau.	1912	f
1124	1126	Murphy, Lloyd C.	sing.	1892	m
1125	1127	Murphy, Henry L.	husb.	1872	m
1126	1128	" Edgar	son	1901	m
1127	1129	" Rayborn	son	1903	m
1128	1130	" Maude	dau.	1905	f
1129	1131	" Birdie B.	dau.	1909	f
	1132	Murphy, Leander	husb.	1858	m
	1133	" Dolly	dau.	1908	f
	1134	" Ela	dau.	1912	f
	1135	" Cordelia	dau.	1915	f
	1136	" Callie Smith	ward	1902	f
1139	1137	Ned, Ezekiel	husb.	1862	m
1140	1138	" Susan	wife	1862	f
	1139	" Julia	dau.	1902	f
1141	1140	Nick, Chiltoskie	son	1882	m
1142	1141	Notty, Tom Peter	husb.	1869	m
1143	1142	" Nancy	wife	1882	f
1130	1143	Okwatage, Elizabeth	wid.	1831	f
1131	1144	Oocumma, James	widr.	1854	m
1132	1145	" Annie	dau.	1895	f
1133	1146	Oocumma, Wilson	husb.	1878	m
1134	1147	Oocumma, Enoch	son	1889	m
1135	1148	Oocumma, Alex	husb.	1866	m
1136	1149	" Annie	wife	1889	f
1137	1150	" Fanny	dau.	1909	f
1138	1151	(Occumma)[sic] John	son	1912	m
1144	1152	Oosowee, John Jr.	husb.	1877	m
1497	1153	" Sally Saunooke	wife	1878	f
1147	1154	Oosowee, Davis Samuel	husb.	1872	m
1148	1155	" Susie	wife	1877	f
1149	1156	Otter, Andrew	husb.	1871	m
1150	1157	" Sarah	wife	1865	f
1151	1158	" Jackson	son	1899	m
1152	1159	" Matilda	dau.	1901	f
1153	1160	" Ollie	dau.	1903	f
1154	1161	Otter, Allen	husb.	1879	m

North Carolina Eastern Cherokee Census 1915-1922
June 30,1916 Taken by: James E. Henderson, Superintendent
1915-1916   Volume I

Number		English Name	Relationship	Date of Birth	Sex
Last	Present				
1155	1162	" Winnie	wife	1876	f
1156	1163	" Sallie	dau.	1901	f
1157	1164	Otter, Ollie	wid.	1850	f
1159	1165	Owl, Dinah	wife	1861	f
1160	1166	" Enoch	son	1899	m
1161	1167	" Betsey	dau.	190	f
1162	1168	" William	son	1893	m
1163	1169	Owl, Jonah	husb.	1882	m
1165	1170	" Philip	son	1909	m
1166	1171	" Ellis	son	1913	m
	1172	" Baby	dau.	1915	f
1167	1173	Owl, Ammons	husb.	1890	m
1168	1174	" Elizabeth E.	wife	1889	f
1169	1175	" Gertrude E.	dau.	1914	f
1170	1176	Owl, George	sing.	1895	m
1171	1177	Owl, Henry	sing.	1897	m
1172	1178	Owl, Frell	sing.	1899	m
1173	1179	Owl, Thomas	sing.	1905	m
1174	1180	Owl, Charlotte	sing.	1909	f
1175	1181	Owl, David	sing.	1894	m
1176	1182	Owl, Lulu	sing.	1892	f
1177	1183	Owl, John	husb.	1859	m
1178	1184	" Margaret	dau.	1904	f
1180	1185	" Louis	son	1910	m
1181	1186	Owl, Sampson	husb.	1854	m
1182	1187	" Agnes	ward	1895	f
1183	1188	Owl, Johnson	husb.	1878	m
1184	1189	" Stacy	wife	1878	f
1185	1190	" Ernest	son	1910	m
1186	1191	" Joseph	son	1913	m
1187	1192	Owl, Adam	husb.	1860	m
1188	1193	" Amelia	wife	1857	f
1189	1194	" Samuel	son	1897	m
1190	1195	" David	son	1897	m
1191	1196	" Martha	dau.	1900	f
1192	1197	" Quincy	son	1905	m
1193	1198	Owl, William	husb.	1884	m
1194	1199	Owl, Thomas	husb.	1887	m
1195	1200	Owl, Moses	husb.	1889	m
1196	1201	(Owl) John R. Wolfe	s-son	1904	m
1197	1202	" Wm. H.	s-son	1906	m
1198	1203	" Richard C.	s-son	1908	m
	1204	" Jessie	s-dau.	1909	f
1201	1205	Owl, James	husb.	1887	m

Number		English Name	Relationship	Date of Birth	Sex
Last	Present				
1202	1206	" Lloyd	son	1909	m
1203	1207	" Stephenson	son	1911	m
1204	1208	" Charlotte	wife	1884	f
1205	1209	Owl, Allen	husb.	1888	m
~~1206~~	1210	" Martha	dau.	1914	f
	1211	" Noah	son	191	m
1206	1212	Owl, Solomon	husb.	1864	m
1207	1213	" Alfred Bryson	son	1897	m
1208	1214	" Lloyd S.	son	1900	m
1209	1215	" Cornelius	son	1902	m
1210	1216	" Ethel	dau.	1906	f
1211	1217	Owl, William David	son	1907	m
1212	1218	" Dewitt	son	1909	m
1213	1219	" Edward	son	1910	m
1214	1220	" Martha Jane	dau.	1895	f
1215	1221	Owl, Theodore	husb.	1886	m
1218	1222	Owl, Mark	husb.	1892	m
1219	1223	Owl, Belvia S.	wife	1892	f
1220	1224	" Jarrett	son	1911	m
1221	1225	" Oscar	son	1912	m
1222	1226	(Owl) Ralph	son	1915	m
1223	1227	Palmer, Dora Owl	wife	1890	f
1224	1228	" Linford	son	1912	m
1225	1229	" Haddington Davis	son	1913	m
	1230	" Nettie Marie	dau.	1916	f
1226	1231	Panther, Job	husb.	1884	m
1227	1232	Panther, Betty	wife	1858	f
1228	1233	Panther, Mark	husb.	1875	m
1229	1234	" Lindy Littlejohn	wife	1888	f
1230	1235	" Simeon	son	1913	m
	1236	" Albert	son	1915	m
1231	1237	Panther, Annie divorced	wife	1863	f
1232	1238	Partridge, Bird	husb.	1879	m
1233	1239	" Elsie	wife	1874	f
1234	1240	George, Elmo Don	s-son	1903	m
1235	1241	Partridge, Sarah dau. of 1238	dau.	1910	f
1236	1242	" John	son	1911	m
1237	1243	Partridge, Winnie E.	sing.	1886	f
1238	1244	French, Juanita M.P.	dau.	1909	f
1239	1245	" Coleman B.	son	1912	m
1240	1246	Partridge, Moses	husb.	1881	m
1241	1247	" Sallie	wife	1888	f

North Carolina Eastern Cherokee Census 1915-1922
June 30,1916 Taken by: James E. Henderson, Superintendent
1915-1916   Volume I

Number		English Name	Relationship	Date of Birth	Sex
Last	Present				
1242	1248	" Savannah	dau.	1907	f
1243	1249	" Sarah	dau.	1911	f
1245	1250	Parris, Catherine Cole	wife	1884	f
1246	1251	(Parris) Laura May	dau.	1907	f
1247	1252	" Lola	dau.	1912	f
1248	1253	Passamore, Nancy Jane	wife	1878	f
1249	1254	" Thomas M.	son	1902	m
1250	1255	" Charles A.	son	1903	m
1251	1256	" Rosa Cordelia	dau.	1905	f
1252	1257	" Oscar	son	1907	m
1253	1258	" David	son	1912	m
1254	1259	Patterson, Lulu W.	wife	1879	f
1255	1260	" Oldham	son	1902	m
1256	1261	" Almer	son	1907	m
1257	1262	" Alwain	son	1910	m
1258	1263	Patterson, Ella Cole	wife	1877	f
1259	1264	" Alonzo	son	1896	m
1260	1265	" Ethel	dau.	1898	f
1261	1266	" Elizabeth	dau.	1900	f
1262	1267	" Celia	dau.	1902	f
1263	1268	" Hobart	son	1904	m
1264	1269	" Arvil	son	1906	m
1265	1270	" Beadie	dau.	1908	f
1266	1271	" Kenneth	son	1909	m
1267	1272	" Zida	dau.	1911	f
1268	1273	Payne, Thomas	husb.	1845	m
1269	1274	Payne, Oliver Clem	husb.	1892	m
	1275	" Mabel	dau.	1914	f
	1276	(Payne) Claude Harrell	son	1915	m
1270	1277	Payne, Willaim[sic] E.	husb.	1872	m
1271	1278	" Paly E.	son	1896	m
1272	1279	" William A.	son	1904	m
1273	1280	" Lydia M.	dau.	1906	f
1274	1281	" Cynthia	dau.	1908	f
1275	1282	" Gertrude	dau.	1910	f
1276	1283	Payne, James M.	husb.	1877	m
1277	1284	" Rollin T.	son	1898	m
1278	1285	" Albert F.	son	1900	m
1279	1286	" Grace Lee	dau.	1904	f
1280	1287	" Erma	dau.	1908	f
1281	1288	" Carra	dau.	1910	f
1282	1289	" Marjie Eunice	dau.	1913	f
1283	1290	Peckerwood, John	husb.	1848	m
1284	1291	" Rebecca	wife	1863	f

Number Last	Present	English Name	Relationship	Date of Birth	Sex
1285	1292	Peckerwood, Lucy Anne	wid.	1858	f
1286	1293	Peckerwood, McKinley	son	1902	m
1287	1294	Pheasant, John	husb.	1853	m
1288	1295	Pheasant, William	husb.	1883	m
1289	1296	" Rachel Emma	wife	1892	f
1290	1297	" Jacob	son	1911	m
	1298	" Laura	dau.	1915	f
1291	1299	Pheasant, Dora Jane	dau.	1891	f
1292	1300	Porter, Florence	wid.	1863	f
1294	1301	(Porter) Iris	dau.	1892	f
1293	1302	Porter, Dewitt	husb.	1890	m
1295	1303	Powell, Dooga	wid.	1870	f
1296	1304	" Sarah	dau.	1899	f
1297	1305	" Holmes	son	1902	m
1298	1306	" Winnie	dau.	1905	f
1299	1307	" Noah	son	1908	m
1300	1308	Powell, Moses	husb.	1887	m
1301	1309	" Elkiny	wife	1883	f
1302	1310	" Stacy	dau.	1909	f
1303	1311	Powell, Stansill	sing.	1891	m
1304	1312	Powell, John Alvin	husb	1853	m
1305	1313	Queen, Levi	husb.	1871	m
1306	1314	" Mary	wife	1880	f
1307	1315	" Minda	dau.	1896	f
1308	1316	" Abraham	son	1900	m
1309	1317	" Addie	dau.	1902	f
1310	1318	" Melinda	dau.	1905	f
1311	1319	" Lottie	dau.	1907	f
1312	1320	" Dinah	dau.	1909	f
1313	1321	" Lillie	dau.	1912	f
1314	1322	Queen, Simpson	husb.	1873	m
1316	1323	" Sallie	wife	1881	f
1315	1324	" Dlliney[sic]	dau.	1899	f
1317	1325	" Nolan	son	1901	m
1318	1326	(Queen) Mary	dau.	1903	f
1320	1327	" John	son	1909	m
1321	1328	" Rachel	dau.	1910	f
1322	1329	" Lucy	dau.	1912	f
1323	1330	" Jasper	son	1895	m
1324	1331	Raper, Alexander	husb.	1846	m
1325	1332	Raper, William Thomas	husb.	1868	m
1326	1333	" Edgar	son	1895	m
1327	1334	" Verdie	dau.	1897	f
1328	1335	" Daffney	dau.	1898	f

Number Last	Present	English Name	Relationship	Date of Birth	Sex
1329	1336	" Augustus	son	1903	m
1330	1337	" James Curley	son	1904	m
1331	1338	" Wm. Arthur	son	1908	m
1332	1339	" Bertha May	dau.	1910	f
1333	1340	" Windell Efton	son	1912	m
	1341	" Floyd	son	1914	m
1334	1342	Raper, Jesse Lafayette	husb.	1871	m
1335	1343	" Cly Victor	son	1898	m
1336	1344	" Claude Emery	son	1899	m
1337	1345	" Curley Clinton	dau.	1901	f
1338	1346	" Minnie Corrine	dau.	1907	f
1339	1347	" William Cecil	son	1913	m
1340	1348	Raper, Marshall	husb.	1878	m
1341	1349	" Clarence Alwain	son	1898	m
1342	1350	" Clinton	son	1902	m
1343	1351	(Raper) Eva	dau.	1904	f
1344	1352	" Bonnie Bell	dau.	1907	f
1345	1353	" William Taft	son	1909	m
1346	1354	" Rosa Ella	dau.	1911	f
1347	1355	Raper, Martie Alexander	husb.	1893	m
1348	1356	Mull, Effie Leora Raper	wife	1894	f
1349	1357	Raper, Charlie B.	husb.	1876	m
1350	1358	" Denver Lee	son	1898	m
1351	1359	" Delta Clifford	dau.	1900	f
1352	1360	" Pearl	dau.	1905	f
1353	1361	" Homer W.	son	1911	m
1354	1362	Raper, Henry John	husb.	1881	m
1355	1363	" Viola Ellen	dau.	1903	f
1356	1364	" Ivan	son	1905	m
1357	1365	" Delia	dau.	1908	f
1358	1366	" Iril	so	1911	m
1359	1367	Raper, Thomas Martin	husb.	185	m
1365	1368	" Whoola B.	son	1888	m
1366	1369	" Martin T.	son	1888	m
1360	1370	" James	son	1896	m
1361	1371	" Lizzie	dau.	1898	f
1362	1372	" Julia	dau.	1900	f
1363	1373	" Clifton	son	1907	m
1364	1374	" Lula	dau.	1909	f
1367	1375	Raper, William P.	husb.	1880	m
1368	1376	(Raper) Willaim[sic]	son	1911	m
1369	1377	Raper, Lon	husb.	1881	m
1370	1378	" Edna	dau.	1910	f
1371	1379	Raper, Gano	widr.	1883	m

North Carolina Eastern Cherokee Census 1915-1922
June 30,1916 Taken by: James E. Henderson, Superintendent
1915-1916   Volume I

Number Last	Present	English Name	Relationship	Date of Birth	Sex
1372	1380	Ratley, Lucy	wife	1852	f
1373	1381	Ratler, George W.	widr.	1873	m
1375	1382	" Rachel	dau.	1896	f
1376	1383	" Henson	son	1898	m
1377	1384	" Morgan	son	1900	m
1378	1385	" Mindah	dau.	1903	f
1379	1386	" Bessie	dau.	1909	f
1380	1387	" Ammons	son	1911	m
1381	1388	Ratler, John	husb.	1887	m
1382	1389	" Emeline	wife	1886	f
1383	1390	" John West	son	1907	m
1384	1391	" Lucy	dau.	1909	f
1385	1392	" Willie	son	1911	m
1386	1393	Ratler, Nancy	wid.	1855	f
1387	1394	" Jonah	son	1889	m
1388	1395	" Robert	son	1901	m
1389	1396	" Walter	son	1904	m
1390	1397	Ratliff, William	husb.	1873	m
1391	1398	" Elizabeth	wife	1876	f
1392	1399	" Emma	dau.	1902	f
1393	1400	" Jacob	son	1904	m
1394	1401	(Ratliff) Ella	dau.	1907	f
1395	1402	" Jonah	son	1910	m
1396	1403	" Myrtle M.	dau.	1913	f
	1404	" Isaac Watson	son	1915	m
1397	1405	Ratliff, Lawyer	sing.	1880	m
1398	1406	Ratliff, James	husb.	1848	m
1399	1407	Reagan, Hester Lambert	wife	1889	f
1400	1408	" Earnest	son	1908	m
1401	1409	" Polena	dau.	1910	f
1402	1410	" Pollard	son	1912	m
	1411	" Bruce	son	1915	m
1403	1412	Reed, James	sing.	1854	m
1404	1413	Reed, Rachel	wid.	1850	f
1405	1414	" Minda	grdau.	1895	f
1406	1415	Reed, Fiddell	husb.	1875	m
1407	1416	" Addie H. Lee	wife	1895	f
1408	1417	" Josie (Lee)	stdau.	1910	f
1409	1418	Reed, Daivd[sic]	sing.	1861	m
1410	1419	Reed, Peter	widr.	1852	m
1412	1420	" Jimmie	son	1888	m
1413	1421	" Lloyd	son	1888	m
1411	1422	" Cindy	grdau.	1897	f
1414	1423	Reed, William	husb.	1884	m

Number Last	Present	English Name	Relationship	Date of Birth	Sex
1415	1424	" Katie K.	wife	1891	f
1416	1425	" Jackson	son	1909	m
1417	1426	(Reed) Cornelia	dau.	1911	f
1418	1427	Reed, Adam	husb.	1878	m
1419	1428	" Sarah	wife	1864	f
	1429	" Moody	son	1914	m
1420	1430	Reed, Rachel	wife	1884	f
		divorced			
1421	1431	" Johnson	son	1905	m
1422	1432	" Samuel	son	1911	m
1423	1433	Reed, Deweese	husb.	1880	m
1424	1434	Reed, Nannie	wife	1884	f
1425	1435	" Susanne	dau.	1905	f
1426	1436	" Sarah	dau.	1912	f
1427	1437	Reed, Maggie	wife	1850	f
1428	1438	Reed, James W.	husb.	1868	m
1429	1439	" Agnes	dau.	1906	f
1430	1440	" William Elmer	son	1910	m
1431	1441	" Meekerson	son	1911	m
1432	1442	George, Maggie Reed	wife	1888	f
1433	1443	Richards, Mamie Payne	wife	1887	f
1434	1444	" Ruby Kate	dau.	1907	f
1435	1445	" Willard Frances	son	1909	m
1436	1446	" Grace Lara	dau.	1912	f
	1447	" Thomas Franklin	son	1914	m
1437	1448	Riley, James	sing.	1901	m
1438	1449	Roberson, Iowa Isabella	wife	1889	f
1439	1450	" Etta	dau.	1908	f
1440	1451	(Roberson) A.J.	son	1911	m
1441	1452	Roberson, Edward E.	husb.	1877	m
1442	1453	" Charlie H.	son	1905	m
1443	1454	" Geoffrey	son	1908	m
1444	1455	" Henry H.	son	1910	m
1445	1456	" Alvin W.	son	1912	m
	1457	" Bessie Iowa	dau.	1915	f
1446	1458	Roberson, Willie O.	sing	1880	m
1447	1459	Roberson, Thomas L.	husb.	1883	m
1448	1460	" William R.	son	1904	m
1449	1461	" Harley T.	son	1908	m
1450	1462	" Sarah Edith	dau.	1911	f
1451	1463	Roberts, Lottie Smith	wife	1877	f
1452	1464	" Callie	dau.	1902	f
1453	1465	" Walter	son	1904	m
1454	1466	" Fred	son	1907	m

North Carolina Eastern Cherokee Census 1915-1922
June 30,1916 Taken by: James E. Henderson, Superintendent
1915-1916   Volume I

Number		English Name	Relationship	Date of Birth	Sex
Last	Present				
1455	1467	" Lula	dau.	1907	f
1456	1468	" Edna	dau.	1912	f
1457	1469	Robinson, Ellen Raper	wife	1865	f
1458	1470	" Emeline	dau.	1897	f
1459	1471	" Hadley	son	1899	m
1460	1472	Beavers, Fannie Rob.	wife	1894	f
1461	1473	Rogers, Jeanette R.F.	wid.	1847	f
1463	1474	Rogers, William	husb.	1864	m
1462	1475	" Martha Caroline	wife	1870	f
1464	1476	(Rogers) Oscar	son	1896	m
1465	1477	" Villa	dau.	1899	f
1466	1478	" Floyd	son	1902	m
1467	1479	" Astor	son	1905	m
1468	1480	" Inez	dau.	1907	f
1470	1481	Rose, Florence	wife	1872	f
1478	1482	" William	son	1893	m
1471	1483	" Jake	son	1896	m
1472	1484	" Grace	dau.	1900	f
1473	1485	" Nora	dau.	1902	f
1474	1486	" Cora	dau.	1905	f
1475	1487	" Benjamin	son	1908	m
1476	1488	" Thurman	son	1910	m
1477	1489	" Wayne	son	1913	m
1479	1490	Morgan, Bonnie Rose	wife	1891	f
1480	1491	" Agnes	dau.	1912	f
	1492	" Rena	dau.	1914	f
1481	1493	Runningwolfe	husb.	1879	m
1482	1494	" Mollie	wife	1881	f
1483	1495	" Lloyd	son	1899	m
1484	1496	" Ammons	son	1904	m
	1497	" Thomas	son	1905	m
1485	1498	" Sallie	dau.	1907	f
1486	1499	" Callie	dau.	1911	f
1487	1500	" Wm. McKinley	son	1913	m
	1501	(Runningwolfe) Soggy	son	1915	m
1488	1502	Sampson, James	husb.	1853	m
1489	1503	" Sallie	wife	1863	f
1490	1504	" Arch (Cucumber)	ward	1905	m
1491	1505	Sanders, Cudge Ellis	husb.	1861	m
1492	1506	" Polly	wife	1857	f
1493	1507	" Moses	son	1896	m
1494	1508	" Viola (Twin)	grdau.	1910	f
1495	1509	Saunooke, Nancy	wid.	1852	f
1496	1510	" Jim	son	1889	m

Number		English Name	Relationship	Date of Birth	Sex
Last	Present				
1498	1511	" Kane	son	1908	m
1499	1512	" Essick	son	1912	m
1500	1513	Saunooke, William	husb.	1870	m
1501	1514	" Edward	son	1900	m
1502	1515	" Anderson	son	1904	m
1503	1516	" Osler	son	1906	m
1504	1517	" Oowanah	son	1909	m
1505	1518	" Friedman	son	1911	m
1506	1519	" Nettie	dau.	1913	f
1507	1520	" Cora	dau.	1915	f
1508	1521	Saunooke, Joseph	husb.	1872	m
1509	1522	" Margaret	wife	1887	f
1510	1523	" Emma	dau.	1910	f
1511	1524	" Charles Logan	son	1913	m
1512	1525	" Nicodemus B.	son	1912	m
	1526	(Saunooke)Richard Alden	son	1915	m
1513	1527	Saunooke, Stillwell	widr.	1842	m
1517	1528	" Malinda	dau.	1886	f
1523	1529	" Jackson	son	1883	m
1518	1530	" Nan	dau.	1890	f
1522	1531	" Stillwell	son	1891	m
1516	1532	" Emeneeta	son	1894	m
1514	1533	" Cindy	dau.	1899	f
1515	1534	" Lillie	dau.	1906	f
1519	1535	Saunooke, Samuel	husb.	1879	m
1524	1536	Sauve, Minnie E. Nick	wife	1881	f
1525	1537	" Marie Mabel	dau.	1908	f
1526	1538	" Josephine E.	dau.	1909	f
1527	1539	" Joseph Peter	son	1911	m
1530	1540	Sawyer, Allen	husb.	1877	m
		divorded[sic]			
1528	1541	" Kiney	wife	1884	f
1529	1542	" Thomas	son	1906	m
1531	1543	Screamer, James	husb.	1858	m
1532	1544	" Cindy	wife	1882	f
1538	1545	" Kane	son	1892	m
1535	1546	" Soggy	son	1894	m
1533	1547	Screamer, Daivd[sic]	husb.	1891	m
1534	1548	" Elnora F.	wife	1897	f
1536	1549	Screamer, Manus	husb.	1882	m
1537	1550	" Nannie	wife	1877	f
1539	1551	Screamer, Enos	husb.	1866	m
		divorced			
1540	1552	Sequohyah, Zachariah	husb.	1859	m

North Carolina Eastern Cherokee Census 1915-1922
June 30,1916 Taken by: James E. Henderson, Superintendent
1915-1916 Volume I

Number		English Name	Relationship	Date of Birth	Sex
Last	Present				
1541	1553	" Louisa H.	wife	1861	f
1542	1554	" Susan	dau.	1901	f
1543	1555	" Alice	dau.	1903	f
1544	1556	" Minda (Hill)	st-dau.	1898	f
1545	1557	" Noah J.	son	1885	m
1546	1558	Sequoyah	widr.	1847	m
1547	1559	Shakeear, Fidella	husb.	1871	m
1548	1560	" Sallie	wife	1864	f
1549	1561	Shell, John	husb.	1852	m
1550	1562	" Sallie	wife	1860	f
1551	1563	" Hettie (Feather)	ward	1897	f
1552	1564	Shell, Ute	husb.	1878	m
1553	1565	" Mattie	wife	1885	f
1554	1566	" Joseph	son	1902	m
1555	1567	" Joshua	son	1908	m
1556	1568	" Boyd	son	1911	m
	1569	" Lillie	dau.	1916	f
1557	1570	Sherrill, John	husb.	1875	m
1558	1571	" Mollie	wife	1879	f
1559	1572	" Kina (Tramper)	s-dau.	1899	f
1560	1573	" Solemn-Sallie	dau.	1902	f
1561	1574	" Julia	dau.	1906	f
1562	1575	" Samuel	son	1909	m
1563	1576	(Sherrill) Andy	son	1913	m
	1577	" Dinnie	dau.	1915	f
1564	1578	Shuler, Georgia Craig	wid.	1884	f
1565	1579	Simpson, Martha Owl	wife	1877	f
1566	1580	Skitty, Sevier	sing.	1848	m
1567	1581	Smith, Jacob L.	husb.	1879	m
1568	1582	" Olive	wife	1879	f
1569	1583	" Lawrence	son	1907	m
1570	1584	" Charles H.	son	1911	m
1571	1585	Smith, Mary Malvina	wife	1862	f
1572	1586	" Oliver	son	1896	m
1573	1587	Smith, James David	husb.	1878	m
1574	1588	" Lawrence	son	1913	m
1575	1589	" Bertha B.	dau.	1915	f
1576	1590	Smith, Duffy	sing.	1880	m
1577	1591	Smith, Francis Elwood	husb.	1886	m
1578	1592	" Bettie Welch	wife	1881	f
1579	1593	" Victor G.	son	1911	m
1580	1594	" Edgar A.	son	1914	m
1581	1595	" Clifford	son	1914	m
1582	1596	Maney, Charity Smith	wife	1891	f

North Carolina Eastern Cherokee Census 1915-1922
June 30,1916 Taken by: James E. Henderson, Superintendent
1915-1916   Volume I

Number Last	Present	English Name	Relationship	Date of Birth	Sex
	1597	" Shuford Kenneth	son	1916	m
1583	1598	" Richard David	son	1912	m
1584	1599	" James Oliver	son	1913	m
1585	1600	Smith, Noah	husb.	1883	m
1586	1601	(Smith) Earl H.	son	1907	m
1587	1602	" Ella A.	dau.	1909	f
1588	1603	" Grace Rose	dau.	1911	f
1589	1604	Smith, Martha Ann	wid.	1837	f
1590	1605	Smith, Lewis H.	husb.	1846	m
1591	1606	" Nancy	wife	1851	f
1592	1607	Smith, Ross B.	husb.	1840	m
1593	1608	" Cynthia	wife	1852	f
1594	1609	Smith, Samuel A.	husb	1866	m
1595	1610	" Goldman	son	1896	m
1596	1611	" David McKinley	son	1899	m
1597	1612	" Jess H.	son	1903	m
1598	1613	" Margaret	dau.	1911	f
1599	1614	" Mortem	son	1913	m
	1615	" Frank	son	1915	m
1600	1616	Smith, William Blain	husb.	1888	m
1601	1617	" Lucy Ann Davis	wife	1891	f
1602	1618	" Annie	dau.	1911	f
1603	1619	Smith, Joseph M.	sing.	1890	m
1604	1620	Smith, Lorena M.	wid.	1864	f
1605	1621	Smith, Thaddeus Sibbald	husb.	1870	m
1606	1622	" Hartman	son	1898	m
1607	1623	" Mary	dau.	1900	f
1608	1624	" Grace	dau.	1906	f
1609	1625	" Mildred	dau.	1910	f
1610	1626	(Smith) Helen	dau.	1913	f
1611	1627	" Carrie Elliot	dau.	1915	f
1612	1628	Smith Lloyd H.	husb.	1873	m
1613	1629	" Roberson	son	1901	m
1614	1630	" Elizabeth	dau.	1902	f
1615	1631	" Noah	son	1904	m
1616	1632	" Tennie	dau.	1906	f
1617	1633	" John D.	son	1907	m
1618	1634	" Dovi	dau.	1910	f
1620	1635	Smith, George Lewis	sing.	1879	m
1621	1636	Smith, Henry	husb.	1849	m
1622	1637	" Russel	son	1905	m
1623	1638	" Hettie	dau	1907	f
1624	1639	" Myrtle	dau.	1909	f
1625	1640	" Rogers, Wesley Crow	s-son	1901	m

Number		English Name		Relationship	Date of Birth	Sex
Last	Present					
1626	1641	"	" Bessie	s-dau.?	1912	f
1627	1642	"	" Maggie	s-dau.	1893	f
1628	1643	Smith, Roxie		sing.	1884	f
1629	1644	Smith, Thomas		husb.	1882	m
1630	1645	"	Buford Roy	son	1909	m
1631	1646	"	Leaina	dau.	1911	f
1632	1647	"	Hosea Gilbert	son	1913	m
	1648	"	Baby	dau.	1915	f
1633	1649	Smith, John Q.A.		husb.	1870	m
1639	1650	"	James C.W.	son	1894	m
1634	1651	(Smith) Josephine		dau.	1896	f
1635	1652	"	Rosena	dau.	1899	f
1636	1653	"	Bessie	dau.	1902	f
1637	1654	"	Robert S.	son	1904	m
1638	1655	"	Ross B.	son	1908	m
1640	1656	"	Velmer	dau.	1914	f
1641	1657	Smoker, Aggie		wid.	1875	f
1642	1658	"	Willie	son	1899	m
1643	1659	"	Peter	son	1902	m
1644	1660	"	Charles	son	1906	m
1645	1661	Smoker, James		husb.	1890	m
1646	1662	"	Luzene Washington	wife	1894	f
1647	1663	"	Davison	son	1912	m
	1664	"	Owen	son	1914	m
1648	1665	Smoker, Will Sawyer		husb.	1871	m
1649	1666	"	Alkinney	wife	1878	f
1650	1667	"	Moses	son	1897	m
1652	1668	"	Hunter	son	1902	m
1653	1669	"	Lizzie	dau.	1905	f
1654	1670	"	Lucy	dau.	1907	f
1655	1671	"	Martha	dau.	1909	f
1656	1672	"	Huto[sic]	son	1912	m
1657	1673	Smoker, Samuel		husb.	1882	m
1658	1674	"	Stacy	wife	1883	f
1659	1675	"	Bascom	son	1903	m
1660	1676	(Smoker) Ollie		dau.	1905	f
1661	1677	"	Cornelia	dau.	1907	f
1662	1678	"	Bettie	dau.	1909	f
1663	1679	"	Caroline	dau.	1911	f
1664	1680	Smoker, Lloyd		husb.	1871	m
1665	1681	"	Nancy	wife	1858	f
1666	1682	Sneed, William S.		husb.	1862	m
1667	1683	Sneed, Samuel white wife		husb.	1857	m

Number		English Name	Relationship	Date of Birth	Sex
Last	**Present**				
1670	1684	" Annie L.	dau.	1898	f
1671	1685	" Maude E.	dau.	1900	f
1672	1686	Sneed, John H.	husb.	1853	m
1673	1687	Sneed, Manco	husb.	1887	m
1674	1688	" Sherman	son	1912	m
1675	1689	" Lawrence S.	son	1912	m
	1690	" Dakota	son	1915	m
1676	1691	Sneed, Osco	husb.	1879	m
1677	1692	" Thomas Mack	son	1907	m
1678	1693	" Wm. Harley	son	1909	m
1679	1694	" Alma	dau.	1910	f
1680	1695	" James E.	son	1912	m
1681	1696	Sneed, Campbell	husb.	1888	m
1682	1697	" Minda	wife	1890	f
1683	1698	" Carrie	dau.	1909	f
1684	1699	" Ernest	son	1910	m
1695[sic]	1700	" Pocahontas	dau.	1911	f
1686	1701	(Sneed) Claudie May	dau.	1915	f
1687	1702	Sneed, Peco	husb.	1875	m
1688	1703	" Sarah	dau.	1901	f
1689	1704	" Blakely	son	1905	m
1690	1705	" Stella	dau.	1908	f
1691	1706	" Lillian K.	dau.	1910	f
1692	1707	" Woodrow	son	1913	m
	1708	" Ruth	dau.	1914	f
1693	1709	Salonaneeta, Bird	husb.	1842	m
1694	1710	Salonaneeta, Leander	husb.	1865	m
1695	1711	" Annie	wife	1879	f
1696	1712	Kalonuheskie, Edith	niece	1909	f
1697	1713	Salonaneeta, Linda	sing.	1865	f
1698	1714	Souther, Dora Cole	wife	1887	f
1699	1715	" Delpha	son	1909	m
1700	1716	" Hartford	son	1910	m
1701	1717	Spray, Gertrude Henrian	sing.	1887	f
1702	1718	Squirrel, George	husb.	1864	m
1703	1719	" Rebecca	wife	1875	f
1705	1720	" Mary	dau.	1903	f
1704	1721	" Sequechee	son	1900	m
1706	1722	Squirrel, Nancy	wid.	1880	f
1707	1723	" Kimsey	son	1897	m
1708	1724	" Nora	dau.	1899	f
1709	1725	" Dinah	dau.	1901	f
1710	1726	(Squirrel) Daniel	son	1904	m
1711	1727	" Ollie	dau.	1906	f

North Carolina Eastern Cherokee Census 1915-1922
June 30,1916 Taken by: James E. Henderson, Superintendent
1915-1916   Volume I

Number		English Name	Relationship	Date of Birth	Sex
Last	Present				
1712	1728	" Sheperd	son	1908	m
1713	1729	" Abel	son	1910	m
1714	1730	" David	son	1914	m
1715	1731	Satndingdeer[sic],Nancy	wid.	1851	f
1716	1732	" Lowen	son	1883	m
1717	1733	Standingdeer, Wesley	husb.	1857	m
1718	1734	" Nancy	wife	1863	f
1719	1735	Standingdeer, Junaluska	husb.	1882	m
1720	1736	Standingdeer, Carl	husb.	1882	m
1721	1737	" Mary Smith	wife	1884	f
1722	1738	" Cecelia	dau.	1907	f
1723	1739	" Virginia	dau.	1909	f
1724	1740	" Roxanna	dau.	1911	f
1725	1741	" Mary	dau.	1913	f
	1742	" Carl Jr.	son	1915	m
1726	1743	Standingdeer, Andy	husb.	1859	m
1727	1744	" Margaret	wife	1859	f
	1745	Saunooke, Polly	ward	1906	f
1728	1746	Standingdeer, Alexander	widr.	1857	m
1729	1747	Stamper, Ned	husb.	1869	m
1730	1748	" Sallie Ann	wife	1876	f
1731	1749	" Hettie	dau.	1897	f
1732	1750	" Caroline	dau.	1899	f
1733	1751	(Stamper), William	son	1901	m
1734	1752	" Lizzie	dau.	1903	f
1735	1753	" Sarah	dau.	1907	f
1736	1754	" Emma	dau.	1909	f
1737	1755	" Roberson	son	1913	m
	1756	" Maggie	dau.	1915	f
1738	1757	Stiles, Mary E. Payne	wife	1870	f
1739	1758	" Oliver	son	1898	m
1740	1759	" Clem	son	1904	m
1741	1760	" Hal	son	1906	m
1742	1761	" Gilbert	son	1894	m
1743	1762	Burrell, Emma Stiles	wife	1896	f
1744	1763	Stiles, Theodocia E.F.	wife	1880	f
1745	1764	" Rufus Virgil	son	1900	m
1746	1765	" Thomas Luster	son	1898	m
1747	1766	" Cora Alma	dau.	1902	f
1748	1767	" Lloyd	son	1905	m
1749	1768	" Ella	dau.	1907	f
1750	1769	" Wlifred[sic]	son	1909	m
1751	1770	Stiles, Hallie L.	wife	1888	f
1752	1771	" Floyd	son	1910	m

Number		English Name	Relationship	Date of Birth	Sex
Last	Present				
1753	1772	" Sadie Lee	dau.	1912	f
1754	1773	St. Jermain, Nicey I.	wife	1871	f
1755	1774	Suagih, Anna	wid.	1854	f
1756	1775	Suagih ?	husb.	1840	m
1757	1776	(Suagih) Mary	wife	1855	f
1758	1777	Sutaga, Sallie	grdau.	1905	f
1759	1778	Swayney, Laura J.	wife	1858	f
1760	1779	" Luzene	dau.	1899	f
1761	1780	" Calcina	dau.	1894	f
1762	1781	Swayney, Jess W.	husb.	1888	m
		white wife			
	1782	" Laura Josephine	dau.	1916	f
1763	1783	Swayney, Lorenzo Dow	husb.	1878	m
1764	1784	" Amanda	dau.	1902	f
1765	1785	" Frank D.	son	1905	m
1766	1786	" Sherman A.	son	1908	m
1767	1787	" Grace	dau.	1910	f
1768	1788	" Dora N.	dau.	1912	f
	1789	" Chiltoskie	son	1915	m
1769	1790	Swayney, John Wesley	husb.	1883	m
1770	1791	" Alvin walker[sic]	son	1910	m
1771	1792	" Laura Josephine	dau.	1912	f
	1793	" Winona L.	dau.	1915	f
1772	1794	Swimmer, Mary	wid.	1859	f
1773	1795	Swimmer, John	husb.	1877	m
1774	1796	" Lucy Ann	wife	1884	f
1775	1797	" Obediah	son	1906	m
1776	1798	" Grace	dau.	1908	f
1777	1799	" Luke	son	1909	m
1778	1800	" George	son	1911	m
1779	1801	Swimmer, Runaway	husb.	1878	m
1780	1802	" Annie	wife	1883	f
1781	1803	Conley, Linda	sist.	1904	f
		half-sister of 1802			
1782	1804	Swimmer, Thomas	husb.	1855	m
1783	1805	" Annie	wife	1859	f
1784	1806	Tahquette, John	husb.	1856	m
		divorced			
1785	1807	Tahquette, Martha	sing.	1864	f
1786	1808	Tahquette, John Alfred	husb.	1870	m
1787	1809	" Anna Elizabeth	wife	1874	f
1788	1810	" Emily	dau.	1906	f
1789	1811	" Frank Glenn	son	1907	m
1790	1812	" Howard Wayne	son	1909	m

North Carolina Eastern Cherokee Census 1915-1922
June 30,1916 Taken by: James E. Henderson, Superintendent
1915-1916   Volume I

Number		English Name	Relationship	Date of Birth	Sex
Last	Present				
1791	1813	" Amy Elizabeth	dau.	1910	f
1792	1814	" Marion	dau.	1910	f
1793	1815	" Alfred	son	1913	m
1794	1816	" ? Baby	son	1915	m
1795	1817	Tail, Jim	sing.	1841	m
1796	1818	Tailor, Eliza	wid.	1857	f
1797	1819	" Julius	son	1899	m
1798	1820	" Timpson	son	1900	m
1799	1821	" David	son	1902	m
1800	1822	" William	son	1907	m
1801	1823	Taylor, Jack	husb.	1890	m
1802	1824	" Rebecca A.	wife	1896	f
	1825	" Sarah	dau.	1915	f
1803	1826	Taylor, Sallie	wid.	1841	f
1804	1827	Taylor, Julius	husb.	1878	m
1805	1828	" Stacy	wife	1875	f
1806	1829	Taylor, Sherman	husb.	1882	m
1807	1830	" Maggie	wife	1887	f
1808	1831	" Alkinney	dau.	1905	f
1809	1832	" George	son	1909	m
1810	1833	" Eva	dau.	1911	f
1811	1834	" Largie	son	1914	m
1812	1835	Taylor, Jesse	husb.	1866	m
1813	1836	" Stacy	wife	1861	f
1814	1837	Taylor, John	husb.	1891	m
1815	1838	" Nannie Welch	wife	1894	f
1816	1839	" Eva	dau.	1912	f
1817	1840	" Seymore	son	1914	m
	1841	" Annie	dau.	1916	f
1076	1842	Taylor, Lula Meroney	wife	1890	f
1077	1843	" Fred (Meroney)	son	1906	m
1668	1844	Taylor, Mary C. Sneed	wife	1897	f
		white husband			
1669	1845	" Inez Catherine	dau.	1914	f
		grdau of Samuel Sneed			
1818	1846	Teesateskie, John	husb.	1860	m
1819	1847	" Jennie	wife	1860	f
1820	1848	" Welch	son	1898	m
1821	1849	" Lloyd	son	1900	m
1822	1850	Teesateski, Sampson	husb.	1891	m
1824	1851	(Teesateski) Sallie	dau.	1912	f
1825	1852	Teesateski, Jesse	husb.	1887	m
1826	1853	" Polly Bird	wife	1884	f
1827	1854	Bird, Bettie	s-dau.	1901	f

North Carolina Eastern Cherokee Census 1915-1922
June 30,1916 Taken by: James E. Henderson, Superintendent
1915-1916   Volume I

Number		English Name	Relationship	Date of Birth	Sex
Last	Present				
1828	1855	" Solomon	s-son	1903	m
1829	1856	" Lucy Ann	s-dau.	1907	f
1830	1857	" Adam	s-son	1910	m
1831	1858	Teesateski, Sarah	dau.	1912	f
		dau of 1852-1853			
1832	1859	Teesateski, Will	husb.	1853	m
1833	1860	" Nessih	wife	1855	f
1834	1861	" Allen (Ledford)	ward	1905	m
1835	1862	" Steve	ward	1906	m
1836	1863	" Josie	ward	1908	f
1837	1864	Teesateski, Illinois	husb.	1875	m
1838	1865	" Cindy Smoker	wife	1888	f
1839	1866	Teesateski, Noah	husb.	1885	m
1840	1867	" Ella	wife	1886	f
	1868	" Matthew	son	1915	m
1841	1869	" Willie	son	1907	m
1842	1870	" George	son	1910	m
589	1871	Teague, Jesse May Garland	wife	1892	f
1843	1872	Teleskie, Ezekiel	widr.	1853	m
1844	1873	Teleskie, Jesse	husb.	1891	m
1845	1874	" Sallie Littlej'n	wife	1880	f
1846	1875	Littlejohn Garret (Gate)	s-son	1906	m
1847	1876	Tootale, Nancy	sing.	1825	f
1848	1877	Tewatley, Rose	wife	1850	f
1850	1878	" William	son	1875	m
1849	1879	" Kane	son	1886	m
1851	1880	Tewatley, Adam	husb.	1875	m
1852	1881	" Desdemonia Crow	wife	1897	f
1853	1882	Thompson, Enos	widr.	1861	m
1855	1883	" Peter	son	1887	m
1854	1884	" Goliath	son	1898	m
1856	1885	Thompson, Johnson	husb.	1866	m
1857	1886	" Nancy	wife	1868	f
1862	1887	" Simon	son	1894	m
1858	1888	" David	son	1897	m
1859	1889	" James W.	son	1900	m
1860	1890	" Jonanni	son	1903	m
1863	1891	" Jackson	son	1905	m
1861	1892	" Annie	dau.	1906	f
1864	1893	Thompson, Ahsinnih	husb.	1884	m
2176	1894	" Mary E. Wolfe	wife	1884	f
1865	1895	Thompson, Sallie Welch	wife	1879	f
		div. wife of 1893			
2067	1896	" Edward R.	son	1903	m

98

Number Last	Present	English Name	Relationship	Date of Birth	Sex
		child of 1893			
2068	1897	" Nannie H.	dau.	1905	f
		child of 1893			
1866	1898	Thompson, Mary W.	wife	1876	f
1867	1899	" Iowa	dau.	1895	f
1868	1900	" Olin	son	1897	m
1869	1901	(Thompson) Greeley	son	1899	m
1870	1902	" Verdie	dau.	1903	f
1871	1903	" Iris	dau.	1905	f
1872	1904	" Lawrence	son	1909	m
1873	1905	" Willard	son	1911	m
1874	1906	Thompson, Wilson	husb.	1888	m
1875	1907	" Rebecca	wife	1890	f
1876	1908	" Elizabeth	dau.	1913	f
1877	1909	Thompson, Martha W.	wid.	1874	f
1878	1910	" Eilliam[sic] H.	son	1895	m
1879	1911	" Mata	dau.	1897	f
1880	1912	" Minnie	dau.	1899	f
1881	1913	" Elbert	son	1900	m
1882	1914	" Braska L.	dau.	1902	f
1883	1915	" Atha W.	dau.	1903	f
1884	1916	" Jewel	son	1905	m
1885	1917	" Marvin	son	1906	m
1886	1918	" Walter	son	1908	m
1887	1919	Thomas, Rhoda R.C.	wife	1886	f
1888	1920	" Ella Henrietta	dau.	1906	f
1889	1921	" William Harrison	son	1908	m
1890	1922	" Lula C.E.	dau.	1909	f
1891	1923	" James Henry	son	1911	m
1892	1924	" Andrew R.	son	1913	m
1893	1925	" Dallas J.	son	1914	m
1894	1926	(Thomas) Allison M	son	1914	m
1895	1927	" Berdie J.	dau.	1915	f
1896	1928	Timpson, James	husb.	1853	m
1898	1929	Coleman, Leslie	husb.	?	m
		?? white ??			
1897	1930	" Callie T.	wife	1893	f
		dau. of 1928			
1899	1931	" Ida Evelin	dau.	1913	f
1900	1932	Timpson, John S.	husb.	1885	m
1901	1933	" Vestry	dau.	1913	f
	1934	" Elsie	dau.	1915	f
1902	1935	Timpson, Columbus H.	husb.	1889	m
1903	1936	Timpson, James Q.	husb.	1881	m

North Carolina Eastern Cherokee Census 1915-1922
June 30,1916 Taken by: James E. Henderson, Superintendent
1915-1916 Volume I

Number Last	Present	English Name		Relationship	Date of Birth	Sex
1904	1937	"	Lawrence Arthur	son	1909	m
1905	1938	"	Lexie May	dau.	1911	f
1906	1939	Timpson, Humphrey P.		son	1858	m
1907	1940	Toe, Johnson		husb.	1857	m
1910	1941	"	Campbell	son	1870	m
1911	1942	Toineeta, Loney		husb.	1860	m
1912	1943	"	Sallie	wife	1860	f
1913	1944	"	Caroline	dau.	1895	f
1914	1945	"	Solomon (Lossi)	ward	1899	m
1915	1946	"	West	son	1882	m
1916	1947	Toineeta, George		husb.	1883	m
1917	1948	Welch, Lloyd		s-son	1895	m
1918	1949	"	Theodore A.	s-son	1897	m
1919	1950	"	Clarence	"	1899	m
1920	1951	Toineeta, Welch Rich R.		s-son	1903	m
1921	1952	"	Edwin T.	son	1909	m
1922	1953	"	F. Geneva	dau.	1911	f
1923	1954	"	Janet	dau.	1913	f
1924	1955	Toineeta, Nick		husb.	1868	m
1925	1956	"	Bettie	wife	1881	f
1927	1957	"	Suagih	son	1889	m
1926	1958	"	Arneach	son	1893	m
1928	1959	Tollie, Lizzie		wife	1887	f
1929	1960	Tooni, Squinchy		husb.	1840	m
1930	1961	"	Lydia	wife	1856	f
1931	1962	Tooni, Moses		husb.	1889	m
		wife No. 1530 Nannie S.				
	1963	"	Willie	son	1915	m
1932	1964	Tooni, Mike		husb.	1874	m
1933	1965	"	Anna	wife	1876	f
1934	1966	"	Elijah	son	1900	m
1935	1967	"	Nancy	dau.	1903	f
1936	1968	"	Lizzie	dau.	1911	f
1937	1969	Tooni, Joseph		widr.	1856	m
1938	1970	"	Andy	son	1892	m
1939	1971	"	Nicey	dau.	1886	f
1940	1972	Tooni, Jukius		husb.	1876	m
1941	1973	"	Lizzie	wife	1882	f
1942	1974	"	Rachel	dau.	1909	f
1943	1975	"	Lossel	son	1910	m
1944	1976	(Tooni) John		son	1915	m
1945	1977	Tooni, Nancy		wife	1879	f
1946	1978	"	Nannie	dau.	1903	f
1947	1979	"	Isaac	son	1905	m

North Carolina Eastern Cherokee Census 1915-1922
June 30,1916 Taken by: James E. Henderson, Superintendent
1915-1916   Volume I

Number		English Name	Relationship	Date of Birth	Sex
Last	Present				
1948	1980	" Mary	dau.	1899	f
1949	1981	" Winnie	dau.	1909	f
1950	1982	" Ollie	dau.	1913	f
1951	1983	Tramper, Chiltoskie	son	1881	m
1952	1984	" Amineeta	son	1890	m
1954	1985	Ute, Mary	wife	1842	f
1955	1986	Wachacha, Roxie	wid.	1861	f
1964	1987	" Nessie	s-dau.	1881	f
1968	1988	" James	son	1886	m
1969	1989	" Sarah	dau.	1889	f
1961	1990	" Jake C.	son	1893	m
1962	1991	" Nancy	dau.	1893	f
1963	1992	" Posey	son	1894	m
1956	1993	" Susie	dau.	1896	f
1957	1994	" John Wayne	son	1898	m
1958	1995	" Jesse	son	1900	m
1959	1996	" Minnie	dau.	1901	f
1960	1997	" Oney	dau.	1904	f
1965	1998	Wachacha, Jarrett	husb.	1874	m
1966	1999	" Amanda Teesateski	wife	1895	f
1967	2000	" Linda	dau.	1913	f
	2001	(Wachacha) Riley	son	1915	m
1970	2002	Wachacha, Charles	husb.	1890	m
1971	2003	Wahyahnetah, John	husb.	1843	m
1972	2004	" Awee	wife	1853	f
1974	2005	" Sampson	son	1883	m
1973	2006	" Posey	grson	1900	m
1975	2007	Wahyahnetah, Allen	husb.	1874	m
1976	2008	" Sallie	wife	1869	f
1977	2009	Wahyahnetah, William	husb.	1870	m
1978	2010	" Kamie	wife	1877	f
1979	2011	" Maggie	dau.	1901	f
1980	2012	" Samuel	son	1904	m
1981	2013	" Leroy	son	1907	m
1982	2014	" Bertha	dau.	1909	f
1983	2015	" Ethel	dau.	1911	f
1984	2016	" Robert Austin	son	1913	m
	2017	" Helen	dau.	1916	f
1985	2018	Waidsutte, Bird	husb.	1877	m
1986	2019	" Mary	wife	1870	f
1989	2020	Axe, Peter	s-son	1893	m
1987	2021	" Manda	s-dau.	1899	f
1988	2022	" Lee	son	1903	m
1990	2023	Waidsutte, Davis	husb.	1872	m

North Carolina Eastern Cherokee Census 1915-1922
June 30,1916 Taken by: James E. Henderson, Superintendent
1915-1916   Volume I

Number Last	Present	English Name	Relationship	Date of Birth	Sex
1991	2024	" Nancy	wife	1876	f
1992	2025	" Addison	son	1910	m
1993	2026	Waidsutte, Ben	husb.	1862	m
1994	2027	" Kiney	wife	1882	f
1995	2028	" Margaret	dau.	1912	f
1996	2029	Walkingstick, Mike	husb.	1845	m
1997	2030	" Caroline	wife	1856	f
1998	2031	Walkingstick, James	husb.	1885	m
1999	2032	" Lucy Ann	wife	1883	f
2000	2033	Walkingstick, Jasper	husb.	1872	m
2001	2034	" Annie	wife	1883	f
2002	2035	" Mason	son	1903	m
2003	2036	" Willie	son	1907	m
2004	2037	" Maggie	dau.	1905	f
2005	2038	" Adam	son	1909	m
2006	2039	" John	son	1911	m
	2040	" Yetze	son	1916	m
2007	2041	Walkingstick, John	husb.	1850	m
2008	2042	" Walsa	wife	1871	f
2009	2043	Walkingstick, Moses	husb.	1894	m
2087	2044	" Jennie Welch	wife	?	f
	2045	" child (no name)	son?	1916	m?
2010	2046	(Walkingstick) Mike child of 2041	son	1902	m
2011	2047	" Enoch child of 2041	son	1909	m
2012	2048	" Ollie Maud child of 2041	dau.	1912	f
2013	2049	Walkingstick, Owen	husb.	1889	m
2014	2050	" Linda	wife	1884	f
2015	2051	(Walkingstick) Cinda	dau.	1909	f
2016	2052	" Lizzie	dau.	1911	f
	2053	" Rachel	dau.	1916	f
2017	2054	Walkingstick, Bascom	husb.	1889	m
1158	2055	" Sokiney Owl	wife	1889	f
	2056	" William	son	1914	m
2018	2057	Wallace, James	husb.	1878	m
2019	2058	" Tahquette Owl	son	1903	m
2021	2059	" Ramsey, Roxie	dau.	1909	f
1520	2060	Ward, Rachel Saunooke sister of Saunooke S.	wife	1886	f
1521	2061	" Priscilla	dau.	1910	f
2022	2062	Watty, Goolarche	husb.	1877	m
2023	2063	" Nessih	wife	1876	f

North Carolina Eastern Cherokee Census 1915-1922
June 30,1916 Taken by: James E. Henderson, Superintendent
1915-1916   Volume I

Number Last	Present	English Name	Relationship	Date of Birth	Sex
2024	2064	" Stephen	son	1897	m
2025	2065	" Kiney	dau.	1900	f
2026	2066	" Lizzie	dau.	1902	f
2027	2067	" Polly	dau.	1906	f
2028	2068	" Olsie	dau.	1909	f
	2069	" Jessan	son?	1916	m?
2029	2070	Watty	widr.	1835	m
		husbn Uhnahyih-dead			
2031	2071	Watty, Ute	husb.	1865	m
2032	2072	" Mary	wife	1871	f
2033	2073	Washington, Key	husb.	1853	m
		divorced			
2034	2074	Washington, Elizabeth	wid.	1840	f
2035	2075	Washington, Joseph	husb.	1882	m
2036	2076	(Washington) Stella B.	wife	1885	f
2037	2077	" Richard B.	son	1910	m
2038	2078	" Josephine	dau.	1913	f
	2079	" Erma	dau.	1916	f
2039	2080	Washington, Jesse	husb.	1875	m
2040	2081	" Ollie	wife	1875	f
2041	2082	" Luzene (Reed)	s-dau.	1897	f
2042	2083	" Amy	dau.	1905	f
2043	2084	" George	son	1907	m
2044	2085	" Jonas	son	1910	m
2045	2086	Wayne, John	husb.	1862	m
2046	2087	" Jennie	wife	1870	f
2047	2088	Wayne, Will John	husb.	1874	m
2048	2089	" Yehkinnie	dau.	1911	f
2049	2090	Webster, Rachel A.	wid.	1842	f
2050	2091	Webster, Wm. Lawrence	husb.	1872	m
2051	2092	" Jetter Columbus	son	1897	m
2052	2093	" Carrie	dau.	1900	f
2053	2094	" Norma	dau.	1903	f
2054	2095	" Wm. Robert	son	1906	m
2055	2096	" Wm. Lewis	son	1912	m
2056	2097	Welch, John G.	widr.	1844	m
2058	2098	" Mark G.	son	1877	m
2059	2099	" Lottie	dau.	1887	f
2057	2100	" Lucinda C.	dau.	1893	f
2060	2101	Welch, Willie	husb.	1889	m
2061	2102	" Maude F.	wife	1894	f
2062	2103	" Wm. Elliott	son	1915	m
2063	2104	Welch, Jimmy	husb.	1891	m
2064	2105	" Lotty	wife	1891	f

North Carolina Eastern Cherokee Census 1915-1922
June 30,1916 Taken by: James E. Henderson, Superintendent
1915-1916   Volume I

Number Last	Present	English Name	Relationship	Date of Birth	Sex
2065	2106	" Elizabeth R.	dau.	1913	f
	2107	" Andy	son	1915	m
2066	2108	Welch, John	sing.	1894	m
2069	2109	" Mary	sis.	1892	f
2070	2110	Welch, James B.	husb.	1873	m
		separated			
2071	2111	Welch, Sampson	husb.	1858	m
2072	2112	" Lizzie	wife	1865	f
2073	2113	Welch, Epheus	husb.	1883	m
2074	2114	" Stacy	wife	1890	f
2075	2115	" Juna	son	1908	m
2076	2116	" Martha	dau.	1911	f
2077	2117	Welch, Edward	husb.	1885	m
2078	2118	" David	son	1911	m
2079	2119	Welch, Lydia T.	wife	1891	f
2080	2120	" Lucy	dau.	1914	f
2081	2121	Welch, Nannie	wid.	1862	f
2082	2122	" Lucinda	dau.	1883	f
2083	2123	" Moses	son	1886	m
2084	2124	Welch, Davis	husb.	1868	m
2085	2125	" Ned	son	1904	m
2086	2126	(Welch) Lizzie	dau.	1906	f
		has sister Jennie?			
2089	2127	Welch, Martha Wolfe	wife	1889	f
2090	2128	" Calinah	dau.	1913	f
2091	2129	(Welch) James	son	1892	m
		son of 2124			
2092	2130	(Welch) Lizzie Bell	dau.	1914	f
		dau. of 2127			
2093	2131	Welch, Elijah	husb.	1862	m
2094	2132	" Ann Eliza	wife	1859	f
2095	2133	" Jonah (Armachain)	s-son	1895	m
2098	2134	" James Elijah	son	1889	m
2096	2135	" Mark	son	1900	m
2097	2136	" Ollie	dau.	1903	f
2099	2137	Welch, Adam	husb.	1886	m
2100	2138	" Annie	wife	1891	f
2101	2139	" Frank Churchill	son	1908	m
2102	2140	" Russell	son	1911	m
2103	2141	" Charlotte	dau.	1913	f
	2142	" Wilson	son	1916	m
2104	2143	Welch, Corneeta	husb.	1880	m
2105	2144	" Nancy Hill	wife	1892	f
2106	2145	" Charles Davis	son	1913	m

North Carolina Eastern Cherokee Census 1915-1922
June 30,1916 Taken by: James E. Henderson, Superintendent
1915-1916   Volume I

Number		English Name	Relationship	Date of Birth	Sex
Last	Present				
	2146	" Sam Louis	son	1916	m
2107	2147	Wesley, Judas	husb.	1876	m
2108	2148	" Jennie	wife	1858	f
2109	2149	" John (Lowen)	s-son	1895	m
2110	2150	Whippoorwill, Manley	sing.	1884	m
222	2151	Whitetree, R. Floy Burgess	wife	1899	f
		Husb. Western Cherokee			
2112	2152	Wildcat, Daniel	husb.	1881	m
2113	2153	" Elsie	wife	1866	f
2114	2154	Will, John	husb.	1862	m
2115	2155	" Jane	wife	1872	f
2116	2156	" James	son	1903	m
2117	2157	" Alice	dau.	1905	f
2118	2158	" David	son	1907	m
2119	2159	" Luzene	dau.	1909	f
2120	2160	" Nellie	dau.	1912	f
2121	2161	Wilnothi, Simon	husb.	1891	m
2122	2162	" Amanda Tewatley	wife	1890	f
2123	2163	Wilnothi, Lot	widr.	1850	m
2124	2164	Wilnoty, Ned	husb.	1851	m
2125	2165	" Sally	wife	1852	f
2126	2166	Wilnoty, Mink	sing.	1845	m
2127	2167	" Moses	husb.	1881	m
2128	2168	" Julius	son	1909	m
2129	2169	" Elizabeth	dau.	1914	f
2130	2170	" James (Greybeard)	s-son	1901	m
2131	2171	" Sallie	s-dau.	1898	f
2132	2172	Macon, Katherine W.	wife	1886	f
89	2173	Winkler, Selina St. Bates	wife	1894	f
2133	2174	Wolfe, Edward	husb.	1891	m
2134	2175	Wolfe, Standingturkey	husb.	1869	m
2135	2176	(Wolfe), Callie	wife	1873	f
2136	2177	Wolfe, Wm. Johnson	husb.	1877	m
2138	2178	" Joe	son	1902	m
2139	2179	" Addison	son	1906	m
2140	2180	" Lilly	dau.	1909	f
2141	2181	" Eli	son	1911	m
2142	2182	Wolfe, Susan	wid.	1851	f
2143	2183	Wolfe, Ward	husb.	1890	m
2144	2184	" Caroline W.	wife	1899	f
2146	2185	Wolfe, Nancy Lossie	wid.	1853	f
2147	2186	Wolfe, Dawson	husb.	1891	m
2148	2187	" Diannah	dau.	1914	f
2149	2188	Wolfe, Loyd Lossie	sing.	1899	m

Number		English Name	Relationship	Date of Birth	Sex
Last	Present				
2150	2189	Wolfe, Jacob	husb.	1871	m
2151	2190	" Nelcina	wife	1873	f
2152	2191	" Joseph	son	1897	m
2153	2192	" Jesse	son	1900	m
2154	2193	" Alice	dau.	1907	f
2155	2194	" Lucinda	dau.	1910	f
2156	2195	" Abel	son	1903	m
2157	2196	" Jacob	son	1913	m
2158	2197	Wolfe, John W.	husb.	1870	m
2159	2198	" Linda	wife	1873	f
	2199	" Rebecca	dau.	1915	f
2160	2200	" Walker	son	1905	m
		deaf and dumb			
2161	2201	(Wolfe) Salkiny	dau.	1910	f
2162	2202	" Jogohe	dau.	1913	f
2163	2203	Wolfe, Junaluska	sing.	1913	m
2164	2204	Wolfe, Owen	husb.	1884	m
2165	2205	" Susie Armschain	wife	1859	f
2166	2206	Wolfe, Taqua	husb.	1889	m
2167	2207	" Ancie F.	wife	1898	f
2168	2208	" Alice	dau.	1912	f
2169	2209	Wolfe, Moses	husb.	1847	m
2170	2210	" Jane	wife	1861	f
2171	2211	" Jonah	son	1894	m
2172	2212	Wolfe, Joseph H.	husb.	1872	m
2173	2213	" Jennie	wife	1870	f
2174	2214	" Callie	dau.	1898	f
2175	2215	" Polly	sis	1846	f
		sister of 2212			
2177	2216	Wolfe, James T.	husb.	1887	m
2178	2217	" Bettie Smoke	wife	1895	f
2179	2218	" William W.	son	1912	m
2180	2219	" Edwin W.	son	1914	m
2182	2220	Kalonuheskie, Jos.	niece	1906	f
2181	2221	Wolfe, Pearle Margaret	sing.	1888	f
		mother white widow			
2184	2222	Wolfe, Charlie Hicks	sing.	1892	m
		mother white widow			
2185	2223	Wolfe, George Lloyd	husb.	1877	m
		separated			
2186	2224	? " Jessie May	dau.	1909	f
2187	2225	" Charles Ray	son	1910	m
2188	2226	Wolfe, David	husb.	1843	m
2189	2227	Wolfe, Louis Henry	husb.	1872	m

Number Last	Present	English Name	Relationship	Date of Birth	Sex
2196	2228	" Louis David	son	1894	m
2190	2229	" Isabella	dau.	1896	f
2191	2230	" Amanda Jane	dau.	1899	f
2192	2231	" Eliza Pauline	dau.	1903	f
2193	2232	" James Wm.	son	1906	m
2194	2233	" Frederick S.	son	1909	m
2195	2234	" Dessie Cleo	dau.	1913	f
2197	2235	Wolfe, Jowan	husb.	1848	m
2199	2236	Yonce, Nancy S.	wife	1852	f
1073	2237	Youngbird, Rufus	husb.	188	m
2183	2238	" Amanda Wolfe	wife	1890	f
		sister of 2221			
1074	2239	Youngbird, Soggie	sing.	1890	f
		2237 is a brother			
1075	2240	" Yonih	sister	1892	f
2200	2241	" Wesley	brother	1894	m
2201	2242	Youngdeer, John	husb	1856	m
2202	2243	" Betsy	wife	1853	f
2205	2244	" Eli	son	1881	m
		deaf and dumb			
2206	2245	" Jonah	son	1883	m
		deaf and dumb			
2207	2246	" Jesse	son	1887	m
2208	2247	" Stephen	son	1889	m
2203	2248	" Martha	dau.	1896	f
2204	2249	" Moody	son	1899	m
2209	2250	Youngdeer, Jacob	husb.	1872	m
2210	2251	(Youngdeer) Lunsih	wife	1853	f
	2252	Murphy, Joseph Manco	husb.	old?	m
		Tenn. children not en.			
	2253	Lambert, Wymer Holt	son	1915	m
		son of 843 ?			
	2254	Dora ? Lossih, Henderson	son	1916	m
		son of 991 ?			
	2255	Arch, Noah	husb.	1898	m
		omitted previously			
	2256	" Sola	dau.	1916	f
		mother Cinda ?			
392	2257	Rave, Martha Cornsilk	wife	1886	f
		omitted by error			
393	2258	" Morris Washington	son	1913	m
394	2259	" Wilmont Arnold	son	1915	m
	2260	Taylor, Eddie	son	1916	m
		father No. 1829			

www.ingramcontent.com/pod-product-compliance
Lightning Source LLC
Chambersburg PA
CBHW020300030426
42336CB00010B/836